Dropped but Not Broken

Learning to Love From the Inside Out

Paula Harris

iUniverse, Inc.
Bloomington

Dropped but Not Broken
Learning to Love From the Inside Out

Copyright © 2011 by Paula Harris.

All rights reserved. No part of this book may be used or reproduced by any means, graphic, electronic, or mechanical, including photocopying, recording, taping or by any information storage retrieval system without the written permission of the publisher except in the case of brief quotations embodied in critical articles and reviews.

The views expressed in this work are solely those of the author and do not necessarily reflect the views of the publisher, and the publisher hereby disclaims any responsibility for them.

iUniverse books may be ordered through booksellers or by contacting:
iUniverse
1663 Liberty Drive
Bloomington, IN 47403
www.iuniverse.com
1-800-Authors (1-800-288-4677)

Because of the dynamic nature of the Internet, any web addresses or links contained in this book may have changed since publication and may no longer be valid. The views expressed in this work are solely those of the author and do not necessarily reflect the views of the publisher, and the publisher hereby disclaims any responsibility for them.

Any people depicted in stock imagery provided by Thinkstock are models, and such images are being used for illustrative purposes only.

All Scripture quotations marked "NIV" are taken from the Holy Bible, New International Version®. NIV®. Copyright © 1973, 1978, 1984 by International Bible Society. Used by permission of Zondervan Publishing House. All rights reserved.
All Scripture quotations marked "NLT" are taken from the Holy Bible, New Living Translation. Copyright © 1996. Used by permission of Tyndale House Publishers Inc., Wheaton, Illinois 60189, U.S.A. All rights reserved.

Certain stock imagery © Thinkstock.

ISBN: 978-1-4620-6382-6 (sc)
ISBN: 978-1-4620-6383-3 (hc)
ISBN: 978-1-4620-6384-0 (e)

Printed in the United States of America

iUniverse rev. date: 12/20/2011

Also by Paula Harris …

A Woman of All Seasons

Daily Divine Deliverance

Becoming Transformed

A New Way, A New You

Dedication

This book is dedicated first and foremost to my Lord and Savior, Jesus Christ, who is Love. Second, this book is dedicated to those closest to my heart, William (my loving husband); André, Aaron, and Arlen (my three sons); Heather (Arlen's wife); Caeli, Arlen Jr., and Ayden (my grandchildren). Last, but not least, I dedicate this book to Harry Coles (my father) and Vertie Coles (my mother) whose love was used by God to bring me into this world.

Contents

Dedication v
Acknowledgments ix
Introduction xi

Part 1: Lost Love – "The Overall Problem" 1
    Love Turned into Hate 5
    Suffering in Silence 8
    Hostile Heart 12
    Dropped but Not Broken 14
    I Won't Let that Happen Again! 17
    Keeping the Scars 21

Part 2: Loyal Love – "The Vertical Solution" 27
    When Does Love Begin? 29
    Deep-Down Desire 33
    No Substitute for Love 38
    From Rejection to Rejuvenation 46
    One Size Fits All 56
    Yes, You Can 64

Part 3: Love Lens – "The Horizontal Solution" 73
    What Does Love Look Like? 75
    In Word or Tongue 83
    Loved Ones as Idols 87
    Self-Preservation 94
    Having Done All, Just Stand 105
    Love When I Don't Even Trust? 115

Part 4: Love Light – "Daily Living It Out" 123
    Deflection from Devotion 125
    Love without Limits 138
    Faith Versus Feelings 154
    "I Do" 170
    A More Excellent Way 182
    Passionate Purpose 189

Resources 195
Reference 196
Endnotes 197

Acknowledgments

My devoted love and heartfelt thanks go to the Board of Directors (Irvin, Patricia, Penny, and William), ministry coordinators (Annette, Betty, Jane, Louise, Patty, Pauline, and Rachel), prayer partners, and all of the supporters of Transformed Worldwide Ministries who have made it possible to get this book into the hands of women.

With warm affection, I want to thank the extraordinary women who were not ashamed to openly share their stories so that other women may be healed.

I send my love and kisses to my brothers and extended family members on all sides, who I love dearly.

In continued love, I thank Aaron, my son, for helping me with the cross illustrations.

A big hug to my Bible study students who helped me select the title of this book.

A special thanks to Suzanne Birmingham, Lujean Burak, Judy Dockstader, Amanda Jamnicky, Kristen Jensh, Emily Mixon, Arlene Stevenson, Betty Taylor, Midge Weber, and Teresa Weber, who met with me one day to share thoughts on the Faith vs. Feelings material previously taught at one of my annual conferences.

Additionally, I dare not neglect to mention all the friends who surrounded me and spurred me on in the faith. My eternal gratitude is yours!

Introduction

"And because iniquity shall abound, the love of many shall wax cold."

(Matt. 24:12, KJV)

I do not need to tell you that because of the wickedness in the world, love in the hearts of many has frozen over. The body of Christ is not excluded. I am not sitting high and looking low with condemnation, for I have had my share of challenges in this area. This is probably why the Lord has led me to pen a few of the lessons I have learned and am still perfecting. However, if my heart is grieved over the lack of love inside and outside of the church, how our Lord's heart must be bleeding as well.

What is presented in this book works, for it is founded on the Word of God. Furthermore, I have lived it and advised others in accordance with the principles presented and have seen the deliverance that results. I have also seen those who agree with the principles but do not apply them to their lives, and I have witnessed the devastation that results. The majority of the stories contained herewith are true, but fictitious names have been used in reference to the women. Relying on the guidance of God's Holy Spirit, I have presented truths in this book to break the bondages of legalism and lawlessness and lack of love. The veins in your heart will open and flow once again with new life, for the blockage leading to a spiritual heart attack will have been removed. You will have new vigor and strength to love in a way different than before. The days you have left on earth will be sweeter should you decide to take this lifestyle as your own. It is one purchased by Jesus and given freely to all. I do not know if you have been dropped, but I do know it does not necessarily mean you are broken.

Part 1

Lost Love
"The Overall Problem"

Part 1:
Lost Love – "The Overall Problem"

"From the end of the earth I will cry to You, When my heart is overwhelmed; Lead me to the rock that is higher than I."

(Ps. 61:2, NKJV)

Come take a journey that deals with real issues woman are afraid to discuss, fearing they may be stripped of their robe of righteousness in front of others. Yet the dark issues *must* be addressed so they can be exposed to the light of Jesus. Once in the light, He will bring deliverance and healing so you may be set free to *"receive"* and *"give"* love. Come ... let us walk out of the shadows into His marvelous light.

Hosea 10:12 (NLT) says: *"I said plant the good seeds of righteousness and you will harvest a crop of love. Plow up the hard ground of your hearts, for now is the time to seek the Lord, that He may come and shower righteousness upon you."*

What you will read in the first part of this book may be hard to bear. If so, please consider that possibly the hard part of your heart is being plowed up. However, if you will yield and let God do a work on the hard parts of your heart, the verse above says that something wonderful will take place. He will come and plant seeds of righteousness in you. Look at the verse again. When good seeds of righteousness are planted, you will harvest a beautiful crop of love! So let God use this book to plow through any hard areas so you can enjoy the harvest. You picked this book up by God's prompting; now let Him speak to you through its pages.

Additionally, Psalm 107:20 (KJV) says, *"He sent his Word and healed them and delivered them from their destructions."* Should you allow Him to plow up the hard areas of your heart, then He will, by His Word, come and bring healing. Your situation is not too hard for Him. He will bring healing and deliverance to you from the things that have been destroying your love life.

Contained herein are true stories of everyday women telling of the challenges that can unexpectedly erupt in any relationship. Lay aside the romance novels and fairy tales, for relationships take work. It is never too late to step out of the shadows into the marvelous light. Therefore, may each story and the content on each page uncover that you are not alone, that hope is peeping around the corner, and that a beautiful harvest of love awaits you too. A day is coming when you, without reservation, will *love from the inside out.*

One such story is that of Grace, who grew up in a home where her family usually got up on Sunday mornings and went to church together. Her parents and four siblings would sit together on hard pews and sing the hymns of old, and then the children would be sent off to Sunday school. In those early years, Grace did not remember anyone talking about a personal relationship with Jesus Christ. Actually, it did not seem as though they were living out the Bible at home, although they did have devotions.

At some point something changed and her parents decided the children should take the Sunday school bus to church while they stayed at home. During this time, Grace was sexually abused by the Sunday school bus driver. It continued for a while and happened to two other girls who rode the bus with her. Grace never understood why they were selected or why they never told what had happened. Now she had a secret that made her feel very dirty, and it began to make her feel disconnected from her family. She had no idea at the time how the situation with the bus driver would impact her for more than thirty years.

Eventually the family started going to another church, and she was able to stuff down the shameful feelings and tuck them deep inside where she did not have to think of them anymore. At this new church they attended both the summer Bible schools and the tent revivals in the evenings. In addition, sometime during fifth or sixth grade Grace prayed to receive Jesus into her heart. However, a time would come when she would look back and wonder if she did it more because it was expected of her rather than actually understanding what she had done.

During the preteen years she became more unsettled and disconnected from her family. She ran away from home often. At age fourteen she was raped again and told no one. She felt as though she deserved it. She began to believe she was a horrible person, undeserving of love, so she continued to run. By running she was trying to find something to fill the emptiness overtaking her. Her parents knew nothing about the abuse and thought she was just being a rebellious teenager.

Her behavior continued to spiral out of control. She drank and used drugs, trying to mask the horrible way she felt about herself. Finally, she left home for good when she was seventeen. She moved in with her boyfriend at the time, got a job, and finished school. After the relationship with the boyfriend ended badly, she went down a continual path of self-destruction for many years. She did not care what happened to her or even whether or not she was alive.

She had another relationship for about nine months in her early twenties that resulted in pregnancy and giving birth to a daughter. Grace loved being a mother, and, even though she was struggling financially, she felt good. She had this beautiful, amazing baby girl to love who was going to somehow help her redeem herself. She finally felt she had a purpose, and things on the inside calmed down for a while.

However, she discovered nothing in this world could bring the redemption she hungered for. There were many bad experiences before she finally came to a place of sheer despair and utter defeat. She was in her midthirties and feeling so down and overwhelmed that she literally threw herself onto the floor of her bedroom. She cried out in pain and anguish to God—the God she had forgotten about, the God she thought had abandoned her, the God she hoped would now hear and forgive her. As she lay there crying, suddenly she felt God's presence in the room with her. She felt a peace come over her unlike anything she had ever felt before. God took her on a voyage through her past and showed her all the times He had been with her. Although she thought she was alone, He showed her the times when He moved her out of harm's way and literally kept her alive. He confirmed He had a purpose for Grace; and even though she was not sure of what it was, she had a renewed hope that was not there before. She knew now that God never abandoned her. He loved her from the beginning and had a perfect plan for her life. She realized she must love and trust Him in return. While it did not happen overnight, she brought the dark things out into the light and is living to be all He wants her to be.

God brought to Grace's mind an old hymn she used to sing when she was a child. It was the perfect reminder of what He promises us. The song is "Love Lifted Me." She remembers the part in the song that goes, *"Love lifted me, love lifted me, when nothing else could help, love lifted me!"* God's unimaginable, unchanging, awe-inspiring, unselfish, beautiful, and perfect love lifted her up out of a destructive place and revealed to her His perfect love. This is Grace's love story and one she continually thanks the Lord for each day.

Once you understand God's love for you personally, you too will be released from past hurts and know a love beyond anyone's comprehension. *"Praise be to the Lord, to God our Savior, who daily bears our burdens"* (Ps. 68:19, NIV). That is why this book has been written. Do you have relational challenges presently? How sad it would be for you to pick this book up and place it down again only to continue to walk around as one who is dead. You can be freed to live and love again! This is your choice … right now … right here … right at this moment. You can be freed to love again or you can let love turn to hate.

Love Turned into Hate

Wanda homeschooled her four children for many years. It took a lot of dedication and sacrifice. She was committed to a different style of parenting than what she had been raised under. She stared out of the window with tears streaming down her face. Unfortunately, at this point, two of her children had graduated from college, and it seemed all the sacrifice was for naught. They despised their mother and felt she had kept them in a prison. They rarely called her and felt they needed to establish their own way of living. Anger welled up inside as she pondered how their attendance at church was sporadic too. The more she thought about the years of sacrifice compared to the disrespect and ungratefulness, the more she became angry. She was at the point where she was ready to disown them completely. Just the thought of them made her nauseated.

What woman doesn't want to be loved? If not for who she is, then at least for what she does. In either case, she desires to be appreciated. She would like to feel special and set apart in some way. This can be in the realm of being a devoted, Christian, fabulous wife; a great mom; an outstanding single woman; a marvelous grandmother; a terrific boss; or a superb employee. It does not matter … all of us want to feel special by knowing we are loved or appreciated. No matter how hard one may be on the exterior, there is this deep desire inside each one of us to be loved. When we experience gratitude or some expression of love, it encourages us. However, when this becomes absent in our lives, we seem to slide down a slope of discouragement. We appear no more significant than an ant crushed by a person casually walking down the street. Nothing is wrong with having a deep desire for love. It was placed inside of us by God Himself. How we fulfill this desire is what makes all the difference.

Even Christian women can get caught up in fantasies regarding love. You may want a knight in shining armor to come and rescue you from a dungeon of loneliness. Or maybe you are waiting for Cupid to shoot an arrow in your "soul mate," who will love you forever and ever. You may already be bound to a mate and believe there is a tonic he can take that would pump some romantic fluid into his veins. Of course, I am being facetious with these examples, but fantasies will prove to be unreal, and Cupid's arrows are mythical. Have you ever been disappointed by love to the point it led you down a path of hatred? Did Cupid's arrows crash? Remember, Cupid or any romantic fantasy that tries to replace or be a substitute for God's sincere love is going to crash sooner or later. When your hope is placed in something that fails, your heart is made sick. *"Hope deferred makes the heart sick, but a dream fulfilled is a tree of life"* (Prov. 13:12, NLT). No matter how messed up things appear at the moment, they can be changed.

Godly women are not immune to heartbreaks. Did you give your all only to find out later in a relationship you were not good enough or you did not measure up to your lover's expectations anymore? Have you ever been left feeling rejected and alone? Did you fight with all your might, only to discover those deep desires resided in you alone, and there was nothing you could do to reproduce them in him? He just was not interested anymore. When innocently confronted with a blatant judgment of "you are no longer valued," it can lead the gentlest woman down a path of bitterness or rage. It is then that you must make a choice to continue on a path of hate or take a different route. If you do not make a conscious effort to jump off this path, a whirlwind of hate will carry you away. Once you have allowed yourself to be swept away, trying to find your way back can be daunting. It could take years … or it could never happen.

A plethora of problems can turn a heart of love into a heart of hate. There are many forms of abuse—and women being literally battered as well. These are confusing cuddles, where love appears to be present, but is a masquerade for lust or another's selfishness. Lust and love are not the same. They are opposites, just like love and hatred. Love is all about giving, and lust is all about getting. If you have been left abused or battered, you do not have to relinquish your deep desire for love.

Sincere love has been in the shadows waiting all this time for you. Once you learn to open your heart again, it will flood your soul!

You need to have a clear understanding of your God-given desire for love. Not only do you need to understand it, you need to know how to *function* in it for love to reach its ultimate fulfillment. If your heart is shut up or closed in any degree by hurts inflicted upon it, you will need to learn to open it once again. By the end of this book, you will have this understanding and know how to receive and give *"sincere love."*

Charles Spurgeon once said, "He is a swift arrow of love, which not only reaches its ordained target, but perfumes the air through which it flies."[1] I believe he was referring to Jesus. Leave Cupid and all the fantasies alone unless you want your heart to be shattered. They will only turn love to hate in the end. Numerous Christian women are bent over trying to pick up the pieces of their shattered hearts. This is not always their fault. This is why it does not seem to make sense when they have wholeheartedly lived for God. You see, in a fallen world, things can fall apart. Yes, even righteous women can give in to hatred if the pain is severe enough. Some foster hate; others just learn to suffer silently.

Suffering in Silence

Janice was faithful to Michael in every way a woman could be faithful. She supported him in his endeavors, she sacrificed her desires for his, and she made sure he had a clean house and hot dinner when he arrived home each day. She wasn't without flaws, but she gave her all for him.

One day as she was routinely putting away his socks in the drawer, something caught her eye. It was a receipt. Upon looking at it closer, she saw it was for a date and place with which she was not familiar. Her heart sunk as she began to suspect Michael of foul play. This was a piece of the many puzzle pieces that were beginning to paint a picture of unfaithfulness. For a year or so she noticed some peculiarities with Michael. He seemed to be distant and have less time for her, but she kept making excuses for him. He was a great guy and a good provider. Although she worked, she made sure their house was a home for him. He began putting more and more hours into work. He even seemed to be too tired to be intimate most evenings. He was becoming quick-tempered and short with her over the smallest things. He accused her of not trusting him if she asked any questions. He would turn things on her as if she was the guilty one for their lack of intimacy. So, many pieces began to come together to make her suspect he was having an affair.

When the moment came for her to confront him, he repeatedly denied all she was saying. He insinuated she was crazy to even think such a thing. He tore into her accusations to the point she retreated into another room. She was consumed with guilt. How could a godly woman have such demonic thoughts? Nevertheless, several other puzzle pieces began to fall into place, and finally she had a completed picture that could not be denied. When confronted this time, Michael finally acknowledged his unfaithfulness.

Janice is like many women who learn to suffer in silence. The silence can last for a month to years until a woman feels she has enough evidence to confront her mate. Even after the initial confrontation, it may take an extended period of time before she has the guts to let someone else know of the betrayal. There are numerous Christian women who do not feel comfortable in approaching a pastor or another in the church to resolve the problem. The thought of the betrayal becoming public is unbearable. Receiving shame, guilt, hostility, and being labeled and ostracized by those who should love you is just too much to bear. It is an indictment to the body of Christ when a Christian woman in trouble does not feel safe in approaching her Christian sisters or brothers for assistance when she is helpless.

Many Christian women, especially when betrayed by a husband who holds a position in the church or community, will suffer silently for various reasons. It can be pride, where she does not want the exposure of a failed relationship. Other Christian women can be cruel in making statements that she should have been able to keep her husband fulfilled, not knowing the husband could have been married to the best woman walking on planet Earth, and he still would have wandered. It could be she truly loves him and does not want to cause him or his reputation any harm. She may have hope the relationship can be worked out, and if she exposes his sin, others—even in the church—may never look at him the same way. He may lose his position and influence. She may try to protect the children involved so they are not devastated as she has been by his betrayal. She may conclude she can handle it, but the children cannot. Face it, there are Christian women who may need the support or else do not want to give up the comforts he provides, and will suffer silently to continue to receive such support. She learns to live with him because her heart has become hard and calloused as well. Some women are just very private and come from generations of those who never reveal what is taking place in their homes. Their motto is "to do or die!" They will suffer silently until placed in their graves.

You cannot tell everyone your business, but when betrayal takes place in your love relationship it helps to have a Christian sister come along to strengthen you and pray for you. While it is not wise to run to someone with every issue that arises in your relationship, there are severe incidents when soliciting the help of a Christian sister becomes mandatory. You will need someone (of course the Lord) to come alongside of you to gird you up.

When something is kept in the dark and under cover, it appears Satan rejoices. He is the prince of darkness and operates in the realm of darkness and lies. Don't let him deceive you into believing you are better off covering over sin and leaving your mate to spiral down further into sin. A day will come when you are forced to deal with the issue, and it may be that had it been confronted earlier, it would not be as complicated as it is now. This is not a time to turn the other cheek. It is not a time to be in denial as an ostrich with its head hidden underground. First John 1:5 (KJV) states, *"God is light and in Him is no darkness at all."* This should teach us to bring everything out into the light where nothing is hidden. Of course, Hebrews 4:13 (NIV) lets you know, *"Nothing in all creation is hidden from God's sight. Everything is uncovered and laid bare before the eyes of him to whom we must give account."*

Whether something is in the light or the dark, God sees it plainly. So you need to deal honestly and expose it all to the light so the truth can be revealed and dealt with in faith. The quest is to bring it *all* out, but not necessarily to *all* people. Both parties need to flush out all of the sewage that has piled up over time. It may bring more pain and hurt, but it is necessary. For some men, once exposed, it almost becomes a relief. They do not have to sneak and hide anymore. Others will deny any proof you may present. If you have to go alone, get some help. Ask God to direct you to someone who can be trusted. Stop suffering silently … the scavenger lurking in the dark is growing stronger and stronger and will one day pounce upon you with the goal of wiping you out completely. Ask God to help you bring it out of the darkness into His marvelous light. In the light is healing, peace, and restored joy. When you decide to bring it out into the light with a trusted person God has led you to, you will have placed yourself in a position where healing can begin. Faith will sustain you as you work out the kinks in the relationship, whether it continues or not. There are some Christian women who are too quick to leave a marriage or relationship that could have been repaired had they been willing to do what was necessary to mend the damage. Just because infidelity has taken place does not mean you have to get a divorce. By the grace of God, some relationships have become stronger after a time of suffering because both parties are now honestly open and not taking one another for granted as before. God specializes in what is impossible with people.

On the other hand, there are some Christian women who will pay a heavy price for secretly holding on to a lie. Their life begins to be snuffed out as their hair falls out, their nerves are destroyed, their personality changes, their health begins to fail, and they are mentally distraught. They can become codependent and not face the truth about their need for this toxic relationship. They may have a false sense of loyalty to someone who is abusing them, thinking it is the godly thing to stay with him. The longer they stay in this relationship, the more their life will be in jeopardy. If this sounds like you, you need to get help right away. Your pastor or trusted Christian sister may be the one you approach. If you are in between congregations at this time, you may need to call an organization such as Focus on the Family (1-800-A-Family) to get counsel.

You may say, "Paula, it was not my spouse that left my heart shattered; it was my best friend or a family member." Likewise, seek to be reconciled with them by flushing out all that may be in the dark. If they do not desire reconciliation, then you still seek help for yourself. You want your heart to be mended so you will still have the capacity to "give" and "receive" sincere love. Be reminded that Jesus said in Hebrews 13:5 (KJV), *"I will never leave thee, nor forsake thee."* You don't have to suffer in silence, for it will only lead to a hostile heart.

Hostile Heart

Olivia had a vibrant personality. She led the woman's ministry at church and had the respect of all the leadership. She knew the Bible inside out and would give godly counsel whenever requested. She played the piano various Sundays and would serve in other areas when time permitted. She and Jeff were admired as having the perfect marriage, until Jeff left the church with Marshal's wife. Olivia and Marshal were stunned by the disclosure of their spouses' affair. While Marshal was able to pick up the pieces and remain in the church assembly, Olivia made the choice to move out of town.

Olivia, who was thought to have had the perfect life, was now living in a blanket of regret. She reminisced how wonderful Jeff was when they first met and how much it appeared he loved her. What could have changed all of that? She could see how she may have contributed to the breakup, but not to the extent things could not have been worked out. Why didn't he at least put forth some effort to restore their relationship? Why did he give it up so freely? Wasn't she worth it? How could all those years not count for something? How could all they did together just vanish in a puff of smoke? The more she pondered one question after another, the more hostility she felt toward Jeff. How could she have wasted her life on him, out of all the other men she could have given herself to?

Once a love relationship has been ended abruptly, it can lead to a hostile heart. A hostile heart is a sick heart. It overflows with a mixture of emotions such as retribution, anger, and malice. A woman is left with feelings of inadequacy, insecurity, insanity, and inferiority. When a woman has a hostile heart, she may experience a roller-coaster ride of rejection, guilt, depression, defeat, sorrow, shame, resentment, disappointment, lack of trust, and low self-worth. She will remain in this cesspool until she gets sick and tired of being sick and tired. It's not enough to be overwhelmed with the influx of negative emotions; she may even turn on herself with severe criticism for past and present actions. Some Christian women even contemplate taking their own lives. She may feel trapped with no way of escape. It may be hard to complete a sentence, much less know the next step to take. It may feel as if she is the walking dead—not quite feeling as if she is in her body or able to connect with those around her. An almost out of the body experience—if such a thing exists.

As a Christian woman, she knows it's wrong to harbor bitterness or live out hatred. She may, without realizing it, adopt a lifestyle of denial. She may become like a beautiful porcelain doll in church, which appears to be all together on the outside but is rotten and full of maggots on the inside. She settles for the imitation instead of the real thing. Little by little she is imploding right in front of others, who are unaware, as her guise serves as a perfect covering. Since she does not truly like the person she has become, she will find it easy to find fault and disapprove of others. So, eventually she makes matters worse by withdrawing or becoming highly critical of others. This in turn, causes further isolation, and she wonders what is wrong with her that she cannot find love.

You need to know you are not alone and are not the first to experience such trauma. You also need to know you are not crazy or have something wrong with you. You have just come face-to-face with the devastation sin brings into this world. Your experience will allow you to understand better why God had to deal with sin in the human heart and why it will be eliminated one day from your very presence.

This wipeout does not have to hold you captive for the rest of your life. Simmering hostility toward the one who offended you can lead to mental, physical, and spiritual illness. Yes, you have been hit with a Mack truck, but there is still some life in you. Get up! Get up! Dear porcelain one, you were dropped, but not broken beyond repair.

Dropped but Not Broken

Brenda believed she loved God, but it was tainted by an unwholesome fear she had of Him. She always walked upright and did not smoke, drink, or have illicit sex. She tried to live the perfect Christian life, not wanting to displease God in any way. No matter how close she was to her friends, if they wanted to have improper fun, she would not participate. Others in her community would always state how they wished they had a daughter like Brenda.

Barely out of high school, Brenda met and fell in love with Randy. It all happened so fast. She was taken up in a whirlwind of passion and compromise that surprised even her. In her heart she knew she was doing wrong, but something about Randy made her not care at the time. Randy did and said the right things to make her feel so secure that it did not matter if even God Himself were angry with her. Anyway, even though she compromised her sexual integrity, she and Randy were planning to get married.

Then the day came when she had to tell Randy she was pregnant. Randy enjoyed the intimacy but not the revelation of the consequences. Brenda could not understand why he was prolonging things and not marrying her as promised.

Brenda's family did not know she was pregnant, and once Randy's family found out, she was labeled a slut. This was heartbreaking considering her squeaky clean reputation before meeting Randy. They did not know her. How could they say such mean things? Randy's family was comprised of preachers and many church attendees. All she received from them were evil looks, condemning words, and a deep emotional scar that would affect her for years to come.

Dropped but Not Broken

Is not the church a hospital for the sin-sick soul? Religious individuals with a pharisaical attitude nauseated Jesus (Matt. 23:15). To see an individual pretend to know and live for Him and at the same time fasten his or her fangs into others is disgusting. This is not the way of your loving Lord. Jesus is not about religious performance but intimacy in a relationship. The problem is that many who are used to the counterfeit do not know the real thing. You need to know the truth about God's love for you. It will deliver you from Satan's fangs and venom.

Now, with a full-blown belly and no ring on her finger, Brenda would muster up enough strength to go about her daily duties with the whispering and stares of others. This mistake could not be hidden. To maintain at least some dignity with her own family, she relocated to Randy's neighborhood. She and Randy were an item, but he just would not pull the trigger to marry her.

Etched in Brenda's mind was a time when Randy's family's had gathered together for an outing. One of his churchgoing relatives said to her, "Why buy the cow when the milk is free?" The lightning-sharp fangs struck her once again. Once those venomous words penetrated her soul, something died in Brenda that day. Motionless, with tears streaming down her cheeks, she was approached by one of Randy's aunts, who softly spoke some words of kindness to her. Brenda barely heard her voice, for she was numb at that point. Yet, later, somehow God would use this same aunt to restore life into Brenda.

Suffering in silence, Brenda reflected upon the person she used to be. She was smart, vivacious, fun-loving, and full of joy! Everyone was drawn to her and liked being in her presence. She was a strong young lady and was well-respected. She was an overcomer, not one who retreated in defeat. A tidal wave of questions bombarded her mind. How did she get here? What was she thinking? Why would she let this happen? Did Randy not understand the impact of his neglect on her life? It was as if a defibrillator, with its surging amounts of electricity, was placed on her, shocking the daylight out of her with no resuscitation. Where was the salve for her open wounds? How could she get out of this noose placed around her neck? Would she ever regain her respect? Would she find herself laughing again?

That was the day she was placed on the treadmill of performance. She would prove to all she was not a slut! She was a good Christian girl. Randy was the only one she had ever had a sexual relationship with, and it was only because she really loved him. She never would have done so had her eyes been open to see that his flickering love was just a flame of lust.

So with all her might she tried *not* to make any mistakes that would lead to further criticism or rejection. As the years progressed, the noose became tighter and tighter as she strove for perfection in the eyes of others. After Randy finally married her, and they continued to have children, she became the taskmaster of perfection for the entire family. Everyone had to look and perform with perfection to avoid any type of criticism or judgment from others. It was as if they all had to prove her purity.

Of course, no family can survive such an arduous load day in and day out, year after year. So, little by little, her family became unraveled and disclosed to all watching that they were not perfect at all. Brenda's cover was blown. Her glass house was dropped. Nevertheless, even though her house had dropped, it was not broken! For it had landed on the cushion of God's unfailing love.

That same aunt who spoke words of kindness to Brenda previously had encouraged Randy and Brenda to get involved in Bible study. The study of God's Word revealed the love of God that would deliver Brenda's family and cushion them from all the shrapnel of Brenda's plan of perfection. It was His love that brought healing to each family member's soul bit by bit.

The family moved out of the perfect glass house and discovered how to be real people with real flaws. When imposters of Christ came ready to strike with their fangs, God's love would not allow the fangs to penetrate. These imposters would have to close their mouths and retreat back into their dark holes. Now Brenda's identity is not found in a perfect family but in a perfect Savior. She was declared pure by her faith in Jesus Christ. Her sinful mistakes would be remembered no more, and Jesus would finally erase the memory of them from her heart as well. In the meantime, Brenda would have to guard against a new performance trap—the trap of "I Won't Let that Happen Again!"

I Won't Let that Happen Again!

Have you fallen lately? My poor mother-in-law had a terrible fall on ice and broke her ankle. In a split second, she found herself lying flat on the ground in terrible pain. That one fall put her through surgical procedures and months of rehab. I remember her saying, "I won't let that happen again!"

With a sigh, Sylvia placed her keys on the table. She proceeded to take her coat off and hang it up. She had just had an abortion, and no one had a clue she was pregnant. Her parents would arrive home in a couple of days, so she had time to recuperate. Even Daniel did not know he had gotten her pregnant. She burst into tears wondering how she could have been so permissive with her body and reputation. Sternness entered into her thoughts as she declared to herself, "I won't let that happen again!"

When an incident invades your life and causes great pain, if you believe you can prevent it the next time, you will most likely conclude, "I won't let that happen again!" You will take precautionary steps to make sure the incident does not repeat itself. Before you know it, you have shifted into a mode of "self-preservation."

The only problem with self-preservation is that it is all about "self." When a person is wrapped up in "self," there is not much room for anyone else. Your arms are wrapped around your own body, not permitting another to be included in the embrace. You develop a determined mindset that nothing is going to bring you down again. You build a wall of protection around yourself. The only problem with trying to protect yourself from others is that you cannot.

Imagine this happening to you. You were with someone who began to look down into a deep, dark hole. This person was enticed to the point she began to fall into the hole, but when she began to fall this person reached out and grabbed your hand as you were standing next to her. You were pulled down into the hole with this person, even though you had given her a warning beforehand about the hole! You made a decision to trust that she knew the danger of the hole and would not get herself in trouble. So when she grabbed your hand and began to pull you down, it shocked you, as you had no control over her actions. It took you by surprise; you were caught off guard. So you plummeted down into the deep dark hole with her. Once you both crashed to the bottom, you were angry and mad that she had done this to you without even considering your wishes or safety at all. She was only thinking of herself and what she wanted. You were injured and bruised badly. Although she was in the hole with you, you felt alone. You were looking at someone you did not know. As a matter of fact, you felt you needed to be protected from one who was supposed to be your friend. How could she be so inconsiderate? You could not see a way back or out of this dark hole. You were experiencing only darkness, and it was all you could see. It left you feeling afraid and very vulnerable and with no clear hope ahead. You did not feel you could shout for help because then many would know the lack of love your friend had for you and how selfish she was. At the same time, you felt someone would believe it was your fault you both fell into the hole in the first place. If you had been attentive, you would have prevented both of you from falling.

You sink down in despair and physically begin to have no strength at all. To try to recover somewhat, you had to place boundaries between you and the now suspected enemy. Then, finally, you knew you had to bring what was in the dark to the light so Satan could no longer keep you bound. You seemed to be stuck in the mind-set of wanting this all to go away and to wake up from this terrible nightmare, but each time you tried you realized it was real, and you could not shake this off like dirt from the bottom of your shoe. Although you recalled God's Word, it did not have the same intimate connection as before. You were still feeling empty. Nevertheless, you continued to call upon Him. At long last, you had a breakthrough and reconnected with Him. You don't know how, but you felt the oneness and deliverance no counselor on earth could provide. The healing in your heart had begun. You now even had compassion and love for your friend. Not trickling compassion as before, but an overflowing forgiveness and love. The Lord reached down into the deep hole and grabbed your hand to lift you out, and, at the same time, you grabbed her hand and the Lord lifted both of you out of the deep darkness.

That day you began to see clearly again. You could even praise God for having fallen into the hole. The hole showed you the truth about both of you and what the Lord desired for you individually and as friends. That which you were angry and resentful about before, became a platform of praise and thanksgiving. Your Lord had freed you from this dark dungeon to hold you ever close to His bosom.

Can you recall an incident when a spouse, family member, or friend pulled you down into a pit without notice, and you found yourself flat on your back looking up? Now I am not saying this literally happened to you. I am stating this figuratively. The fact they would do such a thing made you declare, "I won't let that happen again!" When you set out to protect yourself, God will let you. But it is better to let God protect you than to expend your own energy to protect yourself and end up in the gutter and more brokenhearted than before.

Lamentations 3:52–57 (NLT) states,

My enemies, whom I have never harmed,
hunted me down like a bird.

They threw me into a pit
and dropped stones on me.

The water rose over my head,
and I cried out, "This is the end!"

*But I called on your name, L*ORD*,*
from deep within the pit.

You heard me when I cried, "Listen to my pleading!
Hear my cry for help!"

Yes, you came when I called;
you told me, "Do not fear."

Are you presently protecting yourself from being hurt again? When you build a wall to keep others out, the same wall will imprison you. You may unconsciously begin to sabotage any intimate relationships. You will begin to be alone, and emotions of loneliness will creep in. It may get to a point it becomes more comfortable to be alone than to be with others. Your self-preservation will keep you locked in. You can look out and see others interacting and enjoying themselves, but you are not able to participate. All you have is self. You will not effectively receive and give love in such a condition. Would you agree? So a campaign of "I won't let that happen again!" will defeat you. It is important to remember that we all get hurt at some point in our lives. These hurts can leave deep scars, but we can keep the scars and still thrive.

Keeping the Scars

When I was a little girl I remember being in a large playroom with my brothers. I loved my four brothers. Even into my adulthood, my brothers were very protective of me—especially my oldest brother, Chuckie. Something went terribly wrong that particular day. My oldest brother was playing with matches, and, without explanation, my long strands of hairs were consumed in fire. In shock, I ran down the hall screaming and unintentionally feeding the flames with oxygen. My poor mother rushed to my aid. Not having enough time to get me to a sink to douse the flames with water, she threw me on a bed and suffocated them. I still remember the smell of burning hair. I don't remember my brother playing with matches after that day. I probably would not think much of it at all had it not been for the scars that remain. I have forgiven my brother, but I am still scarred. I will take the scars with me to my grave. God in His blessed mercy has allowed my hair to grow back to a length that keeps them covered. No one would know unless I revealed them.

Someone may have scarred you to the extent you will have to carry those marks to the grave, but it does not mean you cannot thrive with them! As I said, God made a way out of no way for me, and He will do the same for you. I am convinced no one escapes scars. We are in a fallen world, and sooner or later we are inflicted with pain that can leave scars. It is not *if* we will be scarred, but *how* we will respond after we receive a scar. Some people bounce back right away, while others seem to take more time. We are all different, and it depends on the intensity of the trauma inflicted. I believe it was Bishop T. D. Jakes that said, "We want God to deliver us out of adversity and He wants to develop us in the adversity."

Some scars that are inflicted may not be hidden. They may be exposed for others to see. Even in such cases, they can be used for your benefit and for the glory of God. Jesus still has His scars, and when He returns we will see the nail prints in His wrists (hands) and feet. For someone who does not understand, this may be repulsive. However, for those of us who do understand the reason for His scars, they are symbolic of His love and our freedom.

Only—and I mean only—God's love, not a man's, family's or friend's love, can wholly restore you. Only He can take all the broken pieces and put them back together where some scars may still be noticed, but their negative effect is gone and totally erased. Only when you give ear to the evil one will you focus on how those scars occurred.

You may not like your scars, and you may wish they would disappear, but they are a part of your testimony. Our battle scars in life can be the very things that help us to learn how to receive and give love all the more. They may have taught us how to relate to another and comfort them with the love we have received (2 Cor. 1:3–6). God has a way of using them in peculiar ways to show forth love. After all, Jesus willingly received His scars to set all of us free who were captives. Let His love give new meaning to your scars. He will give you new eyes to see the beauty of them.

I will explain in this book how you can know this love and be set free by it. For it was not until I gained a true understanding of God's love for me that I began to live again, scars and all. I now know how to love from the inside out.

As warned, we have plowed up some hard ground in this part of the book. We see a Christian woman can have a love relationship turn into hate, leaving her to suffer in silence. If she suffers too long, she may develop a hostile heart and treat others with bitterness. Yet, if she begins to understand she was dropped but not broken, she can recover. One thing she has to be careful of is trying to control her circumstances by declaring, "I won't let that happen again." The very relationships she craves will be stymied by a controlling personality as much as by a bitter one. She will have to acknowledge her scars. She understands hiding or denying them will get her nowhere. Instead, with a mustard seed of faith, she can embrace her scars, for they will be used to give her a greater capacity for sincere love.

Now proceed on your journey to the next part of this book, "Loyal Love," that you may experience the healing and the crop of love you deeply desire. The disappointments in your life up to this point can be redeemed by God to produce such a wondrous testimony beyond your imagination. You cannot see it yet, but He is molding you into the woman He wants to use to encourage others and to give Him glory. You can indeed become a fountain of love that refreshes everyone who comes in contact with you. So let's continue your journey of moving out of the shadows into His marvelous light. Revelations 12:11 (KJV) states, *"And they overcame him by the blood of the Lamb, and by the word of their testimony."*

Smile; Jesus loves you!

Part 2

Loyal Love
"The Vertical Solution"

Part 2:
Loyal Love – "The Vertical Solution"

"The Lord hath appeared of old unto me, saying, Yea, I have loved thee with an everlasting love: Therefore with lovingkindness have I drawn thee."

(Jer. 31:3, KJV)

In Part 1 you took a journey regarding the emotional upheaval of experiencing "Lost Love." A woman does not have to be jilted by a man to have this experience. It can also come by a loved one's death, by divorce, by a loved one moving away, or by whenever a bond is broken or weakened. At some point, life seems to present to each woman a degree of lost love. Yet this life lesson can expand the heart for a greater capacity to love. You do not have to erect barriers to protect your heart from further pain.

The subtitle of this book is, *Learning to Love from the Inside Out*. To "love from the inside out" means the boundless love of Jesus is flowing out of you to others. It means you have *received* His love and are now *giving* it to others. You cannot give what you have not received. So throughout this book I will refer to "loving from the inside out" by using the terms *"receiving"* and *"giving"* sincere love. This love will come from the inside of you out to others. It is a love you may have heard of but not be fully practicing. This "Loyal Love" is needed to keep your heart open to love too. On the following page is an illustration to see the miraculous flow of this love. Still, one needs to know when this love begins.

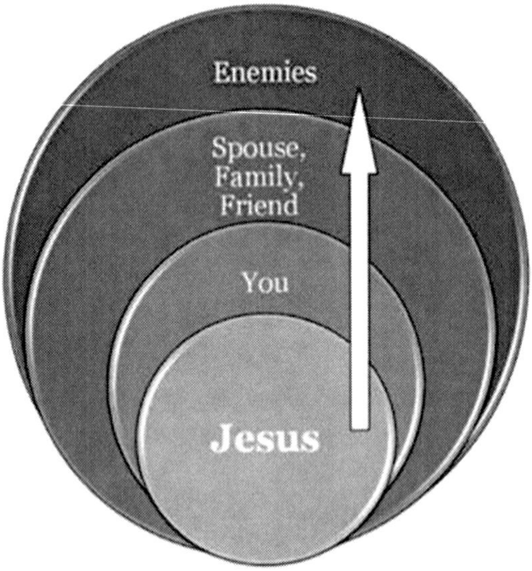
Enemies
Spouse,
Family,
Friend
You
Jesus

When Does Love Begin?

Gwen's heart was beating out of control as she tried to stay focused. He was only holding her hand while everyone gathered in a circle to pray. Why was she falling apart? They were on the same missionary team and loved the outreach to the poor. Somehow, in observing Kevin's care for the underprivileged, Gwen was beginning to grow really fond of him. She always considered him a dear brother in Christ, but now she had entered a new realm of affection. When did her feelings begin to change?

From the beginning of time God has always been involved in a love relationship. When you think about the Trinity, before we were ever created, there was a loving relationship between the Father, the Son, and the Holy Spirit. Sincere love and the intimacy it provides have existed from the beginning in God. The whole Bible is a love letter from a loving God to any who are willing to receive His love. You witness in the Bible a love relationship of giving and receiving that cannot be fully understood with the human mind. To explain the love that exists among the Trinity could take several books in and of themselves. Nevertheless, you can glean some insight from Bible passages as to the love that binds the three together.

The Father's love for the Son has always existed. It had no beginning; neither will it ever have an end. John 3:35–36 (NLT) states, *"The Father loves his Son and has put everything into his hands. And anyone who believes in God's Son has eternal life. Anyone who doesn't obey the Son will never experience eternal life but remains under God's angry judgment."* The Father loves the Son so much He has placed everything into His hands. Anyone who rejects the Son has rejected the Father and will experience the Father's wrath. John 17:1–2 (NLT) states, *"Father, the hour has come. Glorify your Son so he can give glory back to you. For you have given him authority over everyone."* In verse 24 of John 17 you see, *"Then they can see all the glory you gave me because* **you loved me even before the world began**!" Jesus, who cannot lie, has told us the Father loved Him even before the world began.

Jesus also declares in this verse He received an abundance of glory as a result of the Father's love. Jesus openly declared the Father's love for Him in John 15:9 (NLT): *"I have loved you even as the Father has loved me."* You see the existence of eternal love again in John 17:5 (NLT), *"Now, Father, bring me into the glory we shared before the world began."* The majesty, greatness, and power of the Father are shared equally with the Son. You see it in this verse by the expression of "we shared before the world began." John 10:30 lets us know Jesus and the Father are one. Furthermore, 1 John 4:8 (KJV) states, *"God is love."* Please understand God **is** love. Not just that God is loving or that God loves, but that God is love. You can conclude from the previous passages: (1) God is love; God the Father and the Son are one; they are both one in love; and the Father further expressed His love to the Son by putting everything under His authority. There was no jealousy, no conflict, no rivalry, no division—only oneness between the two. This is the way it has been and always will be. This is where love started, or, more accurately, this is how love has always existed.

Likewise the Son has always and will always love the Father. John 14:30–31 (NLT) states, *"I don't have much more time to talk to you, because the ruler of this world approaches. He has no power over me, but I will do what the Father requires of me, so that the world will know that I love the Father. Come, let's be going."* The Son, Jesus Christ, demonstrated His love for the Father by doing everything the Father required of Him. Even to the point of coming down to earth in the form of man that He may die a terrible death by crucifixion, be buried, and then rise the third day from the grave. In doing so, He fulfilled all of the Father's righteous requirements for sin to be forgiven by a Holy God. Why? Because it was the Father's desire to have a love relationship with mankind and not be separated due to His holiness. So Jesus left the presence of a loving Father and all the glory of Heaven to identify Himself with sinful man, so that you and I could be saved from the power of sin. Philippians 2:7–11 (NLT) states, *"Instead, he gave up his divine privileges; he took the humble position of a slave and was born as a human being. When he appeared* in human form, he humbled himself in obedience to God and died a criminal's death on a cross. Therefore, God elevated him to the place of highest honor and gave him the name above all other names, that at the name of Jesus every knee should bow, in heaven and on earth and under the earth, and every tongue confess that Jesus Christ is Lord, to the glory of God the Father." This, my dear, is love! So Jesus's love for the Father was expressed by His obedience to fulfill the Father's plan of redemption. Again, Jesus expressed His oneness with the Father in John 17:21 (NLT), *"I pray that they will all be one, just as you and I are one—as you are in me, Father, and I am in you."* When you read 1 Timothy 1:1 and 2:3 (KJV), they make reference to *"God our Savior,"* showing that God the Father and Jesus our Savior are eternally one.

The Holy Spirit is also an everlasting part of this love triangle. He (not "it") is one with the Father and the Son. Only God is holy, and we call Him by the title of the "Holy" Spirit. In Isaiah 61:1 (KJV) He is referred to as, *"The Spirit of the Sovereign Lord."* In other words, He is one with the Father. If He is one with the Father, He is also one with the Son, as noted previously. In Acts 5:3–4, Peter told Ananias He had lied to the Holy Spirit, and then in the same breath he told him he had not lied to the Apostles but to God—by interchanging Holy Spirit with God, he is acknowledging their oneness. The Holy Spirit's love in the Trinity is expressed by obedience as well. He obediently indwells each person who places their faith in the redemptive work of God through Jesus Christ His Son. This indwelling of the Holy Spirit is assurance that God's presence is with that person no matter what takes place. Some of what the Holy Spirit does in the life of a believer is: He teaches, comforts, empowers, sanctifies, bears spiritual fruit in, gives spiritual gifts to, and illuminates the Word of God to those who are a part of God's family. As a matter of fact, the Word of God is referred to as "The sword of the Spirit" in Ephesians 6:17. Again, He is God with us. All He does is in harmony with and brings glory to Jesus. John 16:13–15 (NLT) states, *"When the Spirit of truth comes, he will guide you into all truth. He will not speak on his own but will tell you what he has heard. He will tell you about the future. He will bring me glory by telling you whatever he receives from me. All that belongs to the Father is mine; this is why I said, 'The Spirit will tell you whatever he receives from me.'"*

So much more can be said about the love between the Father, the Son, and the Holy Spirit (John 15:10, John 3:35, John 5:20, John 10:17, and Matt. 12:18). What has been presented is enough to bear witness to the truth that all three have had and will continue to have a loyal love for all eternity. Love began a long time ago. The more you understand God's love for His Son, the more you will understand how much He loves you by willingly sacrificing Him on your behalf. When you understand the love relationship between them, and how it has always existed, then you can pattern your love relationships after them and understand to a greater degree your deep-down desire for love too.

Deep-Down Desire

Erica glanced down at her watch to see how much time was left before she would depart for lunch. Her two close friends at work were taking her out to celebrate her thirtieth birthday. All she had to do was deliver the completed project to the accounting department and she would be ready to go. While en route to deliver the documents, she reflected over the years that had so quickly passed. She remembered how she always had this deep-down desire to be loved and swept off her feet by Prince Charming. She recalled the dolls she used as a young girl to act out the whole love scene. Here she was approaching another birthday and still no wedding ring. She chuckled at how limited her thinking was back then. God had fulfilled this deep-down desire for love in a way she had never imagined, and it did not include Prince Charming.

Revelation 4:11 (KJV) states, *"Thou art worthy, O Lord, to receive glory and honour and power: for thou hast created all things, and for thy pleasure they are and were created."* Furthermore, Romans 11:36 (KJV) states, *"For of him, and through him, and to him, are all things: to whom be glory for ever. Amen."* The Godhead together has created all things. That includes spouses, family, and friends. It includes everything in the heavens, on the earth, and below the earth. It includes what you can see and what you cannot see—such as spiritual rulers and principalities (Eph. 6:12). God existed before anything else, and He holds all creation together. God, who created all things according to His desire, desires for you to be in relationship with Him and experience sincere love. Jesus prayed in John 17:21 (NLT), *"I pray that they will all be one, just as you and I are one—as you are in me, Father, and I am in you. And may they be in us so that the world will believe you sent me."*

It has already been established that God is love, and the relationship among the Trinity is one of love. To be united with God is to be united to love itself. Mark Guy Pearse once said, "God is love; and it is good, as it is true, to think every sun-ray that touches the earth has the sun at the other end of it; so every bit of love upon God's earth has God at the other end of it."[2] Additionally, 1 John 4:16 (KJV) states, *"And we have known and believed the love that God hath to us. God is love; and he that dwelleth in love dwelleth in God, and God in him."*

This God, who is love, has given you a God-given desire for love. You were created to be in a love relationship with God and others. The rest of your time on earth will be the perfecting of these relationships. It has been recorded that individuals on their deathbeds have regrets due to a lapse in some relationship, not money or prestige. Again, this deep-down desire has been placed in you by God.

According to God's design, there are two main desires that you have in your life: you have a desire to *receive* sincere love, and you have a desire to *give* sincere love. These two desires were designed in such a way that they were to be met in God first and then in others. These two desires or needs are at the root of many relationship quarrels. Adam and Eve's relationship in the garden is a great example of this. Adam and Eve had a desire to receive and give love, and God met that need. They lacked nothing. They did not need clothes; neither did they need to go shopping. Everything was taken care of, but they became dissatisfied once they gave in to Satan's temptation. Eve turned and thought God was withholding something from her and may have thought, "No one is going to deny me; I am going to get my needs met." Only to find out it led to sin and corruption. Adam put his relationship with Eve before God, and he too fell into sin. Both of their desires were corrupted when they selfishly tried to have them met by thinking they knew better than God.

You will make the identical mistake when you think you know better than God how to get your needs met. If you put other people (Luke 14:26) and other things (Matt. 6:19–21) before God, you too will go without your love desires being met. You have probably witnessed Christians in the church who have these deep-down desires, but they are not being met.

In this part of the book, you will gain an understanding of your relationship with God—the vertical desire you have to *receive* love. Later in the book, you will focus on the horizontal desire in regards to *giving* love. God opened my eyes to this truth, and should you decide to live this way, you will bear testimony that this is true as well.

Romans 12:9 (NIV) says, *"Love must be sincere."* What is sincere love? This is not a human or worldly love. It is a love that only stems from God. Note the Scripture says love must be—not should be, not can be—but it must be sincere. When looking up sincere, here are some of the ways in which sincere love is described. As you read this, think about whether you are receiving this type of love or whether you are giving this type of love on a continuous basis. Sincere love is genuine, pure, honest, devoted, truthful, faithful, wholehearted, unconditional, and void of pretention, hypocrisy, and exaggeration. Does that describe your type of love? Do you know what type of love it describes? It describes agápe love. Agápe love is the Greek word for God's love. Only God has the ability to provide this type of sincere love, which is truthfully consistent no matter what takes place. It is not hypocritical; neither is it with any exaggeration. So only God's love, agápe love, is able to be the sincere love just described. It alone can fulfill the need He put in us. It alone provides the ability to *receive* this type of love and to *give* this type of love—to love from the inside out.

Phileo is a Greek word for another type of love. It is a human love you are able to produce. Phileo is where we get the word Philadelphia. It is the type of love between friends. If you have something that is in common with someone else, you may develop a love or a friendship with them. That is phileo love. Now, the only thing is, if phileo love is not ruled by God's agápe love, it can become perverted. That is why some women with their friendships may become involved with lesbianism. Since the friendship did not operate in conjunction with God's agápe love, it became perverted on its own. You see in God's Word that Saul and David had a good friendship, but then Saul got jealous of David. The friendship, without agápe love operating in it, faltered in the end.

There is another type of love: Eros love. Eros love can also be produced by human beings. It is a physical or sexual love. It is designed to be between a man and a woman who are joined in marriage. Yet, we see it is perverted today if it is not again sustained by agápe love. Men and women will get involved sexually even if they are not married. They will even live together if they choose. Some who are single will go to bed just to test the person out to see if that person is fit to marry. If they determine the person is not fit, then they will move on to the next individual. You see again how human love fails in relationship to agápe love? David with Bathsheba is an example of eros love gone awry (2 Sam., chaps. 11 and 12).

There are some single women who are not functioning in agápe love but are exercising all kinds of sexual passion and pleasure outside of marriage. Then, sad to say, there are married women who get to the point where they might say, "All right, come on … your minutes are up … roll over." So we have it all backwards in this society! Married women are the ones who should be free in expressing erotic love, but some do not want to be bothered.

It breaks my heart to hear how some young girls are actually using their cell phones to take pictures of parts of their bodies and texting them to boys. Why would you take a picture of a part of your private areas and text them to somebody else? Relationships become perverted when they are not governed by God's agápe love. Relational breakdowns take place because we do not understand or practice God's agápe love.

There is another type of love—storge love. It is a Greek word for the love you have within a family. It is family love. Joseph's story in Genesis 37:1–35 shows how family love can also be perverted if agápe love is not functioning within the relationship. We also know family members who can live next to or close to one another and not even speak. Even family love can be perverted when agápe love is absent.

God lets us know what agápe love looks like when it is functioning within a relationship. Of course, relationships are made up of individuals. First Corinthians 13:4–8 (NLT) gives us an example of what it looks like when God's love is operating in an individual. *"Love is patient and kind. Love is not jealous or boastful or proud or rude. It does not demand its own way. It is not irritable, and it keeps no record of being wronged. It does not rejoice about injustice but rejoices whenever the truth wins out. Love never gives up, never loses faith, is always hopeful, and endures through every circumstance. Prophecy and speaking in unknown languages and special knowledge will become useless. But love will last forever!"* This agápe love of God never fails! God's love is so different from the human love of eros, storge, and phileo.

God also gives us an example of what it looks like when man is functioning in his human, worldly love. Second Timothy 3:1–5 (NKJV) says, *"But know this, that in the last day, perilous times will come."* Are they here? They are. The economy is one thing, but seeing so many people hurt and shoot each other as if life did not matter, is terrifying. *"For men will be lovers of themselves. Lovers of money."* Is this true? *"Boasters, proud, blasphemers, disobedient to parents."* Are you a parent experiencing this? *"Unthankful, unholy, unloving, unforgiving, slanderers, without self-control, brutal, despisers of good, traitors, headstrong, haughty, lovers of pleasure rather than lovers of God, having a form of godliness but denying its power."* This is quite different from how agápe love operates. [Comments within passages not in italics are mine.]

The Trinity has always functioned in a love relationship. From the beginning of time and for all of eternity, you have been made to function in this love relationship with them. Ecclesiastes 3:11 (NLT) states, *"He has planted eternity in the human heart, but even so, people cannot see the whole scope of God's work from beginning to end."* As a Christian woman, have you been deceived into trying to get your deep-down desire for love met differently from God's design? Are you turning to other people or putting other things ahead of God, thinking they are going to fulfill your God-given need to *receive* and *give* love? Remember what Jesus prayed for in John, chapter 17? Do you think God's heart is grieved when you try to get your desires fulfilled in a different way than His design? Yes, indeed, He is grieved. If your love relationship is lacking with Almighty God, your love relationship will lack on the human level as well. Sincere agápe love does not exist apart from God. Your God-given desires will not be met unless they are fulfilled in God first and *then* in others. When you seek God's kingdom first, all else will be added to you. Matthew 6:33 (KJV) states, *"But seek ye first the kingdom of God, and his righteousness; and all these things shall be added unto you."* This is important for you to remember. Sooner or later, along with the entire human race, you will agree there is definitely no substitute for God's agápe love.

No Substitute for Love

Rebecca had been friends with Agnes for more than twenty years. Now, as she placed the flowers by Agnes's graveside, she reminisced about how both of them used to laugh all the time. Their friendship fit like "a hand in a glove." They were two single women who rejoiced over their singleness. They did not waste one day pouting over the absence of a spouse. Then one day Agnes had a stroke, which led to a severe heart attack that took her life. It was so swift Rebecca could not wrap her arms around the fact that her friend was gone. Even if she made a hundred new friends, not one of them could ever replace Agnes.

There is no need for God to change, for He is perfect in every way. To change would denote some type of improvement or adjustment in Him personally or in His God-given plan. The only thing that may need to change is your viewpoint concerning your God-given deep-down desire for love and how it is to be met. Remember, God's love is so much different from human love. God's love originates and comes from Him. He is the source of agápe love and all sincere love. As humans, we have the capacity to love with eros, storge, and phileo love. We can function in these to some degree apart from God. However, agápe love emanates from God alone. Observe the following chart and note the differences between God's love and human love. An explanation of each characteristic follows the chart.

Dropped but Not Broken

God's Agápe Love	Or	Man's Human Love
is Divine		is Human
is one-sided		is two-sided
self-sacrificing		selfish
unconditional		mostly conditional
voluntary		at times voluntary
eternally unchanged		changes often
immeasurable		can be measured
indestructible		can be damaged / destroyed
universal		discriminating
holy and just		can be evil and unjust
secure and peaceful		insecure and fearful

God's love is divine in origin (1 John 4:20, Heb. 8:10–12, 20). God's love is one-sided. That means whether you believe Him or not, whether you respond to His love or not, He loves you. It doesn't matter what you do. He will not stop loving you because **He is love**. *"Hesed"* is an Old Testament word in reference to God's love. It means He is a covenant-keeping God, is faithful, dependable, keeps His promises, and does the right thing all the time. Our love is two-sided. Whether we want to admit it or not, it is self-conscious. In our subconscious we are always thinking, "I want something"—even if it is only appreciation. If I do something for you out of love, I want you to at least acknowledge it. So, human love is always two-sided. If you continue to give love to someone, and they do not respond in some fashion, sooner or later your love will die or fizzle out. Our type of love is always two-sided. We want something in return. We have expectations. In contrast, God's love is not dependent on how we act or what we think. It just is. His love for us will continue whether we return love to Him or not.

God's love is self-sacrificing (Isa. 53:3–6). God loved you so much that He did not just say it, He demonstrated it by giving up His precious Son, Jesus Christ, to die a violent death in your place so you would be able to be reconciled with Him. This was done for you in spite of your disobedience in getting your desires met in other ways. God sent His most precious Son, Jesus Christ, so you would be able to have a relationship with Him and be reconciled with God. He put His love into action, demonstrating how His love is self-sacrificing. On the other hand, our love is selfish. We want some need met; even sometimes when people get involved in ministry, they do it because it makes *them* feel good. So human love, most of the time, is about us. It is about self. One may say, "Let me do that again, because it felt good."

God's love is unconditional (Rom. 3:23). Again, it is unconditional since you do not have to do anything to gain it. God's love is a free gift, and it is just something he gives to you all the time. It is present for you right now, at this moment. It is not based on your performing. Did you have your devotions this morning? Do you believe God is not going to love you if you neglected to do so? No. His love is not based on performance or conditions. Now, can we say the same about our love? Our love can definitely be based on conditions and on being reserved only if the other person continues to act or think or feel the way we think he or she should act, think, or feel.

God's love is voluntary (Heb. 7:26–27). No one twisted God's arm to just love you. He created you because he delighted in you. Even before your parents knew about you, He knew every intricate thing about you as you were being formed in the womb. Even when you were just a mass of cells, God was delighting in you. So, realize His love is one that is just voluntary. Our love can be involuntary. In reference to family, one might say, "Well, I didn't ask to be born in this family, but it is what it is, and I have to make do. I know she is my sister, but I cannot stand to be in her company." This is a reality for some.

God's love is eternal, and it remains unchanged (Jer. 31:3). His love was from the beginning of time and will continue all the way through eternity. His love will never fail, His love will never stop, and His love will never change. It is not one way toward you one minute and different toward you the next. In contrast, our love may be based on our emotions and our will. You cannot control emotions, for they just spring up. Someone can offend you, someone can make you mad, someone can do all kinds of things to you, and that might affect your level of love toward that person from one minute to the next. So, our love can change from one day to the next.

Dropped but Not Broken

God's love is immeasurable (Eph. 3:14, 19). He will do a multitude of things you cannot begin to even ask or think just to show you He loves you. It is immeasurable. You cannot measure it, and you cannot figure it out; it is immeasurable. Our love can be measurable in that you do a favor for me or you make me feel good, and I'll do the same for you—you rub my back, and I'll rub your back.

God's love is indestructible (Rom. 8:38–39). God's love cannot be destroyed. It says in God's Word, "While we were yet sinners." While you were yet an enemy against God, spitting in His face, going about your own way, thinking you know what is best, God still loved you. You cannot destroy God's love for you. Human love can be damaged or destroyed. If something happens between spouses, or between family members or friends, one can walk away, and that love relationship can be destroyed or damaged.

God's love is universal (John 3:16). God loves all of us. God loves the whole world. Not just a particular set of people and not just a particular race. Our love can be selective and discriminating. You will get close to whom you feel a need to get close to and reject or avoid others.

God's love is just and holy (Rom. 6:23). This is the other side of God's love. God's love is compassionate, full of mercy and grace, but you cannot think about God's love without knowing God is holy, and He has to be just. He has to judge sin. He has to discipline those He loves. Someone who really loves you is not going to sit by while you destroy your life. So God's love is just and holy, and He will discipline His children as it says in the book of Hebrews. He is not like us. We may say, "All right now, Suzy, I told you. Stop that. Don't hit Johnny anymore. What did I tell you? Didn't I tell you, Suzy? Stop hitting Johnny. Now, if you—if you hit him again, I'm going to have to punish you. I am going to punish you! Oh, now you wait until your father comes home. I am telling you. I'm—I'm—don't do it again!" God is not like that. God must deal with sin. He does not just talk about it and not act. God has to, in love, deal with you when you go astray. That is His lovingkindness toward you and His love in helping you not to be harmed by sin. We see again, our type of love can be unjust and very sinful. You can reject a person without having a reason. You may not like the way a person looks, so you withhold your love. You do not like what they said, so you withhold your love.

God's love is secure and peaceful (Heb. 13:20–21). When you understand God's love, you will see it is not dependent on what you do. You can be secure because God is not going to take His love away from you. God's love is always going to be there. Human love can be insecure and fearful. At any moment, you can do something and not even know you messed up with a spouse, a family member, or a friend, and that person can walk out on you. Especially today, Christians are getting divorced just as quickly as nonbelievers. (I understand some divorces are thrust upon women who had no desire to be separated from their spouse.) So please understand why it is important for us to know about this agápe love. It is going to keep us. It is going to be our foundation so when all the other loves fail us (and they will at one point or another), we have a sure foundation to land on. Because of this security, you are not going to be wiped out by the loss of other relationships. His love will provide security and peace.

This is important! Right now you may feel, "Oh, my world is fine. I am not worried about anybody leaving me. I'm not worried about anybody falling out of love with me." Before you know it, in the next minute, you can find out something is not right in a relationship you have with someone that you love dearly. You cannot make a man stop walking out on you. You cannot make a child not turn his or her back on you. You can give your all to a man, and he can still turn around and find someone else to meet his desires. You can raise a child up and give that child everything you think he or she needs so they can have it better than you. Yet, a child can turn his or her back on you in a minute and not even talk to you. This is why it is important to know the sincere love of God!

This agápe love that flows to you from Jesus Christ, God's Son, has to be the stability, the source, the building block for all the other relationships in your life. All these other relationships may fail or disappoint you. Most of us spend all of our time and all of our effort in these relationships—the eros, the storge, and the phileo. You may think "Oh, Jesus understands. I do not have a lot of time for my love relationship with Him. I know He created me to love from the inside out, but I really do not have enough time each day. In today's economy, I have to get out there and make sure my kids have those hundred dollar sneakers. I have to make sure I am able to get some money and go get a lift so that my husband thinks I am still attractive. I found things head south on my body and do not return north again, so I have to get some money to tighten up things. God, you know my family; they are dysfunctional and require all my time. I've concluded I have to spend some time with my friends and have some relief from my daily pressures. So, Lord, you understand. You see all things. I don't have enough time in the day to spend with You." So you put all of your effort and spend all of your time on the other relationships.

It is important to remember that when these other relationships are not held up by His agápe love, they are going to falter. It does not matter—they will, in one way or another, disappoint you eventually. You cannot keep putting all of your time and effort on all the other human relationships without them being tied to a relationship with Him. They have to be an outflow of His agápe love. Then they will become stable. Then all of them will hold up when God's agápe love is filtered through your eros, storge and phileo relationships. They will have God's grace to bring some fulfillment to you, but if you just take them and do not have agápe love, they will fail. They will not hold up.

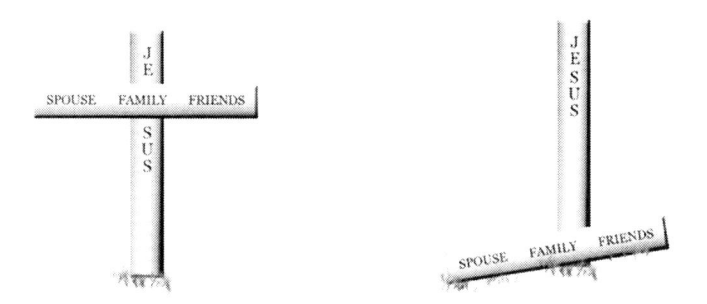

Let me use the cross as an illustration of how all the relationships in our lives should relate one to another. Picture your love relationship with Jesus as the vertical piece of wood. (Jesus is representative of the Trinity: Father, Son and Holy Spirit.) This vertical piece of wood is secured in the ground. Now picture all your other relationships—spouse, family, and friends—as the horizontal piece of wood. Now picture yourself holding the horizontal piece (all other relationships) up to the vertical piece of wood (relationship with Jesus). If you let go of the horizontal piece of wood, what happens? It crashes to the ground. The reason for it doing so is because it was not fastened to the vertical piece of wood (which will not crash to the ground). Are you getting this picture? Do you see the significance of the horizontal being attached to the vertical? Then when a spouse, a family member, or a friend disappoints you, the love of God will hold you up and be there to keep you. Not only that, but regardless of what others do, you will have the capacity to love them unconditionally.

The scriptural basis for this illustration is Matthew 22:34–40 (NIV), *"Hearing that Jesus had silenced the Sadducees, the Pharisees got together. One of them, an expert in the law, tested him with this question: 'Teacher, which is the greatest commandment in the Law?' Jesus replied: 'Love the Lord your God with all your heart and with all your soul and with all your mind.' This is the first and greatest commandment. And the second is like it: 'Love your neighbor as yourself.' All the Law and the Prophets hang on these two commandments."*

We must make time for our love relationship with God. I am not saying we do not need to spend time on building up our other relationships. What seems to be the norm is the other relationships are all we live and work for at the neglect of developing our relationship with Jesus. Everything we have worked for can be gone in a moment's time. It can fall to the ground just as the horizontal piece of wood did. Yet, when these relationships are being sustained by God's agápe love, they will hold up, being fastened to His love.

When you live like this, should one of the horizontal relationships (viewing the cross illustration) let you down, you will not have lost your identity or your value. For your identity and value are determined by the vertical relationship you have with Jesus. If the husband leaves, or if the children go and establish their own homes, you will still recognize your value, because it is derived primarily from the vertical not the horizontal relationships. Some women place their all in the horizontal relationships, and when they crash to the ground, their own self-worth is gone. Even if a spouse dies, they feel they have nothing to live for.

Jesus is able to come into a marriage where adultery has taken place and give the grace for you to forgive. That family member who acts nasty toward you every holiday will be surprised to hear you say, through His agápe love, "How are you doing? You sit here; I will get it for you." In

God's love, you are still able to minister to them—not wanting anything in return, for this is how God's love functions. He will be able to come into a friendship where your friend ran her mouth and give you the grace to say, "It's all right, come on. Let's get back together."

Your other relationships are beautiful when they are tied into your relationship with Jesus. Begin to view your other relationships as an added blessing. They are like the peanut butter in a Reese's cup. They are like the peppermint in a Peppermint Patty. They are an added blessing. You will be amazed at how life will take on new meaning when your other love relationships are upheld by your love relationship with God. Living in this manner will change your relationships from continual feelings of rejection to rejuvenation.

From Rejection to Rejuvenation

Iris was multitalented and very popular in her community. Everyone seemed to feel she had it all together. She seemed to be able to dress like a princess one moment and then be in dirty overhauls the next to accomplish a task. She seemed flawless and capable of achieving anything she set her mind to. Little did others know that within she was very insecure and fought constant feelings of rejection that would often overwhelm her.

She had agreed to be on a committee at the church and was anticipating a great time of serving and being with the other ladies. Others seemed to always place upon her this unspoken code: "You do everything right! We are counting on you!" This, of course, led to Iris having the pressure to not fail and to be exact and perfect in everything. The stress of trying to be perfect, or at least better than what she perceived of herself, made her susceptible to live according to others' opinions of her. This is a crazy way to live, for people's perceptions change as swiftly as the direction of the wind. Galatians 1:10 (NIV) states, *"Am I now trying to win the approval of men, or of God? Or am I trying to please men? If I were still trying to please men, I would not be a servant of Christ."*

There are situations that can produce a performance mentality in you that produces a self-inflicted prison. Marcy always tried to give the appearance of being the perfect homemaker. When it was time for her husband to return home from work, she would rush around and make sure the house and children were neat and tidy. The only problem was it made her a nervous wreck. Her husband's coming home only signaled anxiety for her each day. Yet, she continued the behavior, taking pride in having a place for everything and everything in its place.

Jocelyn was a supervisor on her job and had six people she was responsible to manage. As a Christian woman she wanted to portray Christ but be down to earth as well. She wanted to win the respect and admiration of her group. Her goal was to be the type of person her coworkers would want to support as head of their department. Jocelyn had placed heavy demands on herself and was running ragged trying to live up to unrealistic standards.

Mollie was a single mom and felt guilty most of the time for not modeling the perfect Christian family. She stressed in trying to be the model single mom. Having a son with no man in her life complicated her efforts. It was a goal she never seemed to reach.

Many Christian women can become workaholics in serving others, whether in the home, community, or at church. Christian women may unknowingly try to mimic the Proverbs 31 woman by striving to do everything right. This, of course, is an unrealistic expectation, as she is not in control of her circumstances or other people in her life.

Belinda has an attitude of "I don't care what anyone else thinks of me." She believes she is doing the best she can, and it is all that matters. Her life, house, and schedule are chaotic, and she can care less. Her belief is that her lifestyle is no one's business but hers and God's. She does not accept criticism or suggestions. Things are done her way, or others can just take the highway. This too is an extreme and can be a form of bondage.

Jackie can be sick herself and will continue to go nonstop to meet the needs of others. She does not want to disappoint others and especially does not like to be involved in any conflict. She is constantly tired but feels obligated to go until she drops.

Christian women are not immune to the trap of performance. If you listen to their conversations, you will hear the guilt and shame of not being good enough or not adequate enough or not meeting the qualifications for certain things they face in life. Not only do they get an F in handling life situations, but also in their Christian walk. They feel they are not good enough when they do not read their Bibles, or when they are not involved in several ministries at the church, or when their husbands or children do not have a fire for God as some others do. They talk as if God has given them an F on their spiritual report cards. Does God give Fs? Does God require us to perform? What work does He require of us?

In John 6:28–29 (NIV) we read, *"Then they asked him, 'What must we **do** to do the works God requires?' Jesus answered, 'The work of God is this: to **believe** in the One he has sent.'"* Wow! Is it really that simple? All we have to do is believe? Look further. We are to believe "in the One He has sent." That is Jesus Christ and His atoning work on our behalf. When you grasp this truth, it will deliver you and set your heart free. It will rejuvenate your life! You will not easily believe God is angry with you or upset with you all the time. You will not accept condemnation and rejection so easily. You will know the Holy Spirit convicts of specific sins, and He does not hurl accusations of condemnation to the children of God recklessly. It is a change of focus from what **we can do** to what **Jesus has already done**.

Any acts of performance that make you feel acceptable to God apart from Christ are nauseating to God. All of your deeds are as filthy rags (Isa. 64:6). The term "filthy rags" is a reference to bloody, stinky, menstrual cloths. God has given a vivid picture of what He thinks of our works offered up to Him apart from His Son. Women of the past could especially understand what it was like to have menstrual cloths. They did not have the convenient pads and tampons women use today. They used pieces of cloth. Furthermore, these cloths did not have any fragrance or deodorizing agent added. Although this may be gross to picture, it is a clear, vivid picture given so that women can easily remember. Picture several menstrual *cloths* that were used during that time of the month, and then picture them stored or piled up. Would you like to have a pile of these placed in your lap? Then why should you believe God would like for you to place a pile of these in His lap? Did He not let us know our works, apart from Christ, are as these stinky, filthy rags? Then why do we insist on making God view our personal works of acceptance as something totally different than these rags? He told us how He views anything we do to be accepted apart from Christ. A lifetime of your good deeds could not gain you acceptance or brownie points with God at all!

Let me give you another vivid picture so this lesson stays in your mind and heart. Picture a little toddler being potty trained. He is so

Dropped but Not Broken

happy and proud of his movement in the potty-chair container that he wants you to be proud of him too. So he picks up what he produced with his bare hands and brings it to you with delight on his face. You, in turn, may be grossed out and not respond with excitement when you see and smell what he is carrying in his hands to offer to you. Although you understand as a mother what he is trying to do through his actions, what he produced and presented to you must be disposed of quickly. God knows your heart when you present your works of acceptance to Him. However, it is what Christ has done on your behalf that makes you acceptable to Him. Your personal works must be disposed of just like the substance produced in the potty.

This lesson is crucial for you to learn. Before you were born, and still in your mother's womb, God's love was involved in molding you and keeping you. This was before you could lift a finger to *do* anything! God is love and has always loved you. Romans 5:8 lets us know even while we were enemies of God and sinning against Him, He still demonstrated His love for us. You have worth and value apart from what you do. If you depend upon your works for acceptance, how would you know if you had met your quota of good works for the day? If you did not meet a particular quota at any given time, then you could experience rejection. Instead, rejuvenation can be experienced by resting in the finished work of Jesus Christ on your behalf. His work has thoroughly made you acceptable and complete in Him (Col. 2:10). It is a blessing to be set free from performing or trying to produce for God.

Think of the thief that hung on the cross next to Jesus. When he placed his faith in Jesus, he did not have the opportunity to come down and do any works or perform any deeds. Yet, Jesus told him that very day he would be with Him in paradise (Luke 23:32–43). It was his belief in Jesus, and not his works, that allowed him entrance into Heaven.

As a matter of fact, Christ's anger was displayed toward those who tried to be accepted by their performance. The Pharisees and Sadducees (religious leaders) of Christ's day were rejected because they felt their works made them acceptable to God. This is referred to as religion. Religion is any form of man working to make himself acceptable to God. Instead, what God desires is a relationship—this is Christianity. The two are very different. In Christianity, God has completed the work necessary to restore us back to Himself. God took the initiative to reach down to us in love. All we need to do is respond positively to His love. Religion is man reaching up to God; Christianity is God reaching down to man. Furthermore, if God does not demand performance from you to be acceptable, you must not let anyone put you in a performance trap to be made acceptable to them. It does not matter who they are.

There is definitely no substitute for the love of God. He has provided everything needed for you to have an intimate relationship with Him. He does not want you to feel rejected but rejuvenated by His love.

A better understanding of the Old and New Covenant will drive home this point as well. In 2 Corinthians 3:5–6 (NLT) we read, *"It is not that we think we are qualified to do anything on our own. Our qualification comes from God. He has enabled us to be ministers of his new covenant. This is a covenant not of written laws, but of the Spirit. The old written covenant ends in death; but under the new covenant, the Spirit gives life."*

This Scripture makes reference to two covenants God had established with His people. One ends in death and the other in life. J. M. Davies contrasts the old written covenant (letter) with the new covenant of the Spirit:

> *This ministry of the "letter" that killeth is illustrated in the 3,000 killed at Sinai, at the inauguration of the Old Covenant (Exodus, chapter 32), and the ministry of the Spirit, the life-giving ministry, is illustrated in the 3,000 saved on the day of Pentecost (Acts, chapter 2).*

The Old Covenant was two-sided—God and man. If you will do "this and that," then I will do "this and that." When you read Exodus 20 you see the words *"you shalt not"* constantly. It was a covenant of performance and works. The people were blessed or punished based on their performance. However, it was always intended by God to be a temporary system to make people aware of their sins and to turn to the Savior who could deliver them from all sin.

In contrast, the New Covenant we live under now because of Jesus Christ is not a two-way covenant. It is a one-way covenant—all God. God is not demanding anything of us to make us acceptable before His sight, but He is saying, *"I will. I will. I will."* God is talking about what

He is going to do. He is not talking about what *you* will do, but what *He* will do. When you look at this passage, He is starting here with Israel, but these particular blessings are available to the church body. That means you! (Be mindful that not all promises to Israel are for the church body today.) Hebrews 8:10–12 (NLT) states, *"But this is the new covenant I will make with the people of Israel on that day, says the Lord: I will put my laws in their minds, and I will write them on their hearts.* (It is not going to be on tablets of stone anymore.) *I will be their God, and they will be my people. And they will not need to teach their neighbors, nor will they need to teach their relatives, saying, 'You should know the Lord.' For everyone, from the least to the greatest, will know me already. And I will forgive their wickedness, and I will never again remember their sins."* [Parenthetical material is mine.] Observe again the words, *"I will, I will."* Who is accomplishing the work? If He says, "I will," how can He not do so? Numbers 23:19 (NLT) says, *"God is not a man, so he does not lie. He is not human, so he does not change his mind. Has he ever spoken and failed to act? Has he ever promised and not carried it through?"* Go back and answer these questions for yourself. If God has said something, we can have confidence it absolutely will be carried out!

Read 2 Corinthians 3:5–6 (NLT) slowly again: *"It is not that we think we are qualified to do anything on our own. Our qualification comes from God. He has enabled us to be ministers of his new covenant. This is a covenant not of written laws, but of the Spirit. The old written covenant ends in death; but under the new covenant, the Spirit gives life."*

Let's reword this passage by inserting "you" into it. It is not that you think you are qualified to do anything on your own. You know your qualification (to be acceptable before God) comes from God Himself. He has enabled you to be a minister of His New Covenant. This is a covenant not of written laws (the Ten Commandments or law given to Moses), but of the Spirit (the Gospel of Grace provided by Jesus Christ). The Old Written Covenant ends in death (brings death to all who break the law), but under the New Covenant, the Spirit gives life (the breaking of the law is forgiven, so there is not death but life).

It cannot be said enough, when you grasp hold of this truth, you will move from a constant mind-set of rejection to a continual mind-set of rejuvenation. You will stop trying to perform to be accepted by God and others, and you will rest in the finished work of Jesus on your behalf. It will help you to understand and accept God's love and provision for you. When you do so, then you will be able to love others as well. Additionally, you will not require others to perform to be accepted and loved by you. They will be released from rejection and move to rejuvenation as well. In every area of bondage, you will see a continual cycle of moving from rejection to rejuvenation in your own life and in that of those you are in relationship with by the power of the Holy Spirit, who brings life. Romans 8:2 (NKJV) says, *"For the law of the Spirit of life in Christ Jesus has made me free from the law of sin and death."*

Now getting back to the previous passage, it tells us the Old Written Covenant ends in death because it condemns everyone who does not keep the law perfectly. So you can perform 99½ percent of the law perfectly but still be condemned eternally for not keeping it 100 percent. The entire human race has been found guilty of not keeping the written law 100 percent (Rom. 3:23). The only man who walked this earth who kept the law 100 percent was Jesus Christ (yet, without sin). Therefore, the entire human race is under God's wrath and deserves death for not keeping His law. *"Cursed is everyone who does not continue in all things which are written in the book of the law, to do them"* (Gal. 3:10, NIV).

The law is not evil. It was written on tablets of stone by God and given to Moses for the people to know when they had sinned (1 Tim. 1:5–17). Its purpose was to reveal sin. By the law is the knowledge of sin (Rom. 3:20). We would not know we have sinned if the law was not established to let us know. The law was intended to bring the knowledge of sin and to convict us of sin. It was not established to *remove* the sin it revealed. Thank God for letting us know when we step out of line. It is good to know when our actions and attitudes are offensive to Him. How terrible it would be to go day in and day out not knowing if you placed yourself under God's wrath or if you displeased Him in some way. God's wrath is a result of Him being holy and having to righteously judge all sin. He would not be holy if He allowed sin in His presence. Since the law was given by God, it too is holy, just, and good (Rom. 7:21). The other great benefit of the law is that it brings us to the end of ourselves (Gal. 3:24). We are convicted of our sin but cannot do anything about it. The law only reveals sin. It does not remove our sin. So we are left in a position of being convicted and under God's wrath.

God would be justified in punishing us for our sin by putting us to death (Rom. 6:23).

In contrast, the New Covenant is of the Spirit and brings life. The law reveals sin in your life, then it convicts you of sin, and then it places you under the wrath and punishment of God. Since you are guilty of sin and of trespassing the law of God, He would be just in sentencing you to death. However, under the New Covenant He has made provision for your sins to be forgiven and forgotten. Jesus Christ, God's only beloved Son, came and took your sins upon Himself. So then He took God's wrath upon Himself, taking the punishment you deserved upon Himself. He died and was buried. The glorious thing is He did not remain dead but rose again the third day, having victory over death and all sin. Now everyone who places their faith and trust in His work is freed from God's wrath once for all. So now they become totally acceptable to a Holy God, since their sins have been removed from them and paid for. Also, His wrath against that sin has been satisfied by it being poured out totally upon Christ. So now Jesus has been punished for our sins (past, present, and future). We do not fear God's wrath will come against us anymore.

Not only did Jesus remove our sins from us (Ps. 103:12 and Heb. 10:17), He has put His robe of righteous upon us (Isa. 61:10). So when God looks at us now, all He sees is the righteousness of His Son. We are covered in Jesus's righteousness. We are made holy and acceptable to God by the *finished work of Jesus on the cross.* It is not by any works of righteousness we have or will ever do (Eph. 2:8–10). We are acceptable before God because of His beloved Son (Eph. 1:6). So, to try to work hard or perform to be acceptable to God is a very offensive act, for it declares the finished work of Jesus on the cross was not enough. It means you are trying to complete or perfect what Christ has already done on your behalf. It means that somehow in your mind His work was left incomplete, and you are unconsciously determined to complete it yourself by your good works!

Every time you think you are doing something to make God love you more, you have crossed the line and declared that Jesus's work on your behalf was not enough. We must really think this through over and over again. It is a continual temptation and must be quenched to have victory over guilt and condemnation. Satan would love for you to have a mind-set of constant guilt and shame. How can God be angry with you when His wrath (anger) was poured out completely on Christ? Your sins were completely and fully judged on the cross. God passed judgment on Jesus, who **fully paid** your debt. Would it not be wrong for Him to then turn around and have you pay what was already paid? He is not unjust in this way. However, our actions seem to portray we believe He requires us to pay too.

When you feel constantly judged by God, you will not be able to live in the fullness of His love. You will always feel you are not good enough or what you do is not acceptable before God. Sooner or later you will become frustrated or angry with Him and rebel or give up. When you fully believe what Christ has done for you (by completing the work and making you acceptable before God), you will be able to have peace and rest in this area of your life.

You may say, "Well, all I have to do is receive Christ's work for me on the cross, and then I can live my life in any way I want." No! Further in this book, you will learn how a true understanding of what Christ did for you will lead you to be sensitive to not continue in a lifestyle of sin. God has provided the perfect solution for our sins once and for all.

John 1:17 (NIV) states, *"For the law was given through Moses; grace and truth came through Jesus Christ."* The law under the Old Covenant could not bring forgiveness of sin and eternal life. That came only by the finished work of Jesus Christ under the New Covenant. The law commanded us to obey and condemned us to death if we did not do so. It told us what was right but did not give us the power to do what was right. It revealed to us we were sinners, but it could not save us from our sins. Thanks be to God that grace and truth came through Jesus Christ! Jesus did not come to the world to condemn us (John 3:17). Instead He came to save all who could not save themselves. He took the very enemies of God and made them not only acceptable to God, but His children and a part of His family. That is grace (all of God's wonderful blessings that we do not deserve). Not only did grace come by Jesus, but truth as well. John 14:6 (KJV) states, *"Jesus saith unto him, I am the way, the truth, and the life: no man cometh unto the Father, but by me."* God, who is holy, could not lavish His abundant blessings upon us (His grace) and deny truth. If He were to deny the truth about sin, He would cease to be holy, which is impossible for God. Although He loved all of us who sinned and therefore were declared sinners by the law, He could not condone or act as if our sin did not exist. Being holy, He had to judge sin and deal truthfully with it. Since the wages of sin is death, He Himself died to pay the penalty of death that we deserved. He did this in agápe love while upholding truth in all His holiness. The book of Romans so beautifully explains the sacrificial love of God. Romans 5:20–21 (NLT) states, *"God's law was given so that all people could see how sinful they were. But as people sinned more and more, God's wonderful grace became more abundant. So just as sin ruled over all people and brought them to death, now God's wonderful grace rules instead, giving us right standing with God and resulting in eternal life through Jesus Christ our Lord."*

Remember, the work is **finished**. It is complete. Jesus came to fulfill the law. There is nothing you can do to add or take away from what Christ has done. Your biggest challenge will be to receive His work for yourself and to place His robe of righteousness on you so you can stop trying to please God by what *you* do. You need to rest in what He has already done on your behalf through His Son. Your Christian walk is not about the work you do but about the relationship that is maintained with your Lord. This is what is being attacked every second and must not be allowed, on your behalf, to slip out of sight. The beautiful thing about this robe of righteousness is that one size fits all.

One Size Fits All

Mona had to learn early in life how to fend for herself. She couldn't stand women who appeared weak or needy. She had always been self-sufficient. She would do her own home repairs and would even fix her car by herself. She was pretty proud of her accomplishments. It was hard for Mona to connect with others in a group. She liked to feel in control, and when others were involved, she could not always anticipate what they may do. Others always seemed to complicate the simplest matters. She cherished the idea of being different and separate. She did not want to be a cookie-cutter person. When Dee shared the Gospel with her and encouraged her to be a part of God's family, she had a hard time accepting the family concept. How could all of these different people become one family? It baffled her at first, but the more Dee shared, the more the Holy Spirit opened Mona's eyes to see the beauty of being one with Jesus. It was a Wednesday evening when Mona put on Jesus's robe of righteousness and found it truly was a one size fits all. Since then, she has never regretted her decision.

When a garment is labeled "one size fits all," rarely does the garment indeed fit all sizes. Nevertheless, the truths presented in this section do indeed apply to all. That is, to all who will receive these truths by faith (having confidence that what God says is true). It doesn't matter whether you have a Bentley in the driveway or whether you live in a shack. God doesn't love one better than the other. You know you have received these truths when you take the robe of righteousness, provided by Jesus Christ, and you put it on yourself. Here is what you need to know to do this very thing that will change your love life forever.

Agápe love will always be expressed in some type of action or sacrifice. Always! God is not just going to say it and not demonstrate it. He has definitely demonstrated his love for you personally. Jeremiah

31:3 (KJV) says, *"The Lord has appeared of old to me saying, yes, I have loved you with an everlasting love. Therefore, with lovingkindness, I have drawn you."* Every day, the Lord is drawing you to Himself and saying, "I love you. I love **you**. I am forever drawing you with my love." Are you hearing His voice? Have you turned to Him and received His love? Have you exchanged your robe of personal performance for Christ's robe of righteousness? Only the children of God are able to wear this robe of righteousness.

John 1:12-13 (NKJV) states, *"But as many as received Him, to them He gave the right to become children of God, to those who believe in His name: who were born, not of blood, nor of the will of the flesh, nor of the will of man, but of God."* To have a child, there has to be a physical birth. To have a child of God, there must be a spiritual birth. This spiritual birth is referred to as salvation. For you to be reading this book, you had to be born physically. To finish this book and walk away knowing how to live in God's agápe love, will take you to be born spiritually. Only by God's agápe love can you truly love God, yourself, and others.

John 1:13, which we just read, tells us three ways in which this new birth (salvation) does *not* take place and the *one way* in which it does. Here are three ways in which we are not born spiritually:

1. Not of blood—A person does not become a Christian or child of God by having Christian parents. Christianity is not passed down from parent to child through the bloodstream.
2. Not of the will of the flesh—No one has the power in his own flesh to produce this spiritual birth. Although you must be willing to receive this spiritual birth, your own will is not enough to provide this spiritual birth.
3. Not of the will of man—No other person, regardless of his or her will for you, can produce this spiritual birth for you. No one else on earth has the power to produce this divine birth in you.

"But of God" is the only way whereby anyone can become a child of God and experience this spiritual birth. These three words tell us the power to produce a spiritual new child remains in God alone and no one else. The three previous points can be used of God to work together with what He is doing to produce a spiritual birth in you, but ultimately only God is able to "give birth" to a child of His. Remember, only the children of God are able to wear Christ's robe of righteousness and stop trying to create their own robe of righteousness and acceptance before God. This *one* robe of righteousness will fit *all* who accept it by faith. Whether one loses or gains weight spiritually, the robe will always fit and never decay. Once the robe is placed on by faith, it can never be taken away from you. "By faith" just means to believe and trust what God has said and to have absolute confidence He will do what He says He will do. You must believe the following truths of what God has said to wear this robe of righteousness.

Romans 3:23 (KJV) says, *"For all have sinned and come short of the glory of God."* God loves you, but you have sinned. This has created a problem with your relationship with God. Ezekiel 18:20 (KJV) lets us know the soul that sins shall die. Isaiah 59:2 says, *"But your iniquities have separated between you and your God and your sins have hid his face from you, that He will not hear you."* So God loves you, but you have sinned. Since you have sinned, you are under the wrath of God and should die. Your sins have separated you from God, so that is hindering you from having that love relationship He designed for you to have with Him. Romans 6:23 (KJV) says, *"For the wages of sin is death."* The only payment you are going to get for remaining in that type of sinful condition is death. Now don't lay the book down … stay with me … this is going to lead to your deliverance and to having the capacity to *receive* and *give* love—to love from the inside out. It may sound harsh at the moment, but the ending is too beautiful to miss. So sin leads to death. When you think of death, think of separation. Death occurs when the spirit is separated from the physical body. Death also occurred when you have sinned, and it caused a spiritual separation between you and God (who is Spirit). Your relationship with God was put to death, but God didn't intend for it to remain that way. The Bible says the gift of God is eternal life through Jesus Christ His Son. God does not want you to be separated from Him. *"When Adam sinned, sin entered the world. Adam's sin brought death, so death spread to everyone, for everyone sinned"* (Rom. 5:12, NLT).

So what did He do? Romans 5:8–9 lets you know God demonstrated His love toward you while you were still sinning. During the time you were committing sinful acts against Him, and were seeking to have your needs met without Him, you were acting as an enemy of God. Yet, He still executed a plan to restore you back into a right relationship with Him.

The Gospel of John 3:16–17 (KJV) states, *"For God so loved the world that He gave his only begotten son, that whosoever believeth in Him shall not perish but have everlasting life. For God sent not his Son into the world to condemn the world; but that the world through Him might be saved."* God loves you. He does not want you to be separated from Him. He wants you to have a love relationship with Him. So what did He do? First Peter 3:18 (KJV) says, *"For Christ also hath once suffered for sins, the just* (Jesus being just and holy) *for the unjust* (you are unjust)." For what purpose? *"That He might bring us to God, being put to death in the flesh, but quickened by the Spirit."* Do you see that? It is Jesus who brings us to God. [Comments within passages not in italic are mine.] It continues in Romans 5:9 (NIV), *"Since we have now been justified by his blood, how much more shall we be saved from God's wrath through him!"*

First Timothy 2:5 (KJV) states, *"For there is one God and one mediator between God and man* (there's only one) *and that's the man Christ Jesus."* Please listen. Don't let your mind stray. Romans 10:9–10 (NLT) says, *"If you confess with your mouth that Jesus is Lord and believe in your heart that God raised him from the dead, you will be saved. For it is by believing in your heart that you are made right with God, and it is by confessing with your mouth that you are saved."*

So, please realize God didn't just say He loved you. He sent Jesus, His only begotten Son, to take your sin and God's wrath upon Him. He died in your place. That is how much God loves you, and that is how much He demonstrated His love for you. You could not pay your sin debt, but Jesus paid your sin debt so you could be set free from sin. So here it is. God loves you, but you have in some form or fashion sinned. Since God is holy and He is just and He has to deal with sin, you came under His wrath. You should have been punished by being put to death, but God did not want sin to separate you from Him. Remember, He created you to have a love relationship with Him. He had to deal with the sin. So He sent His only begotten Son, Jesus Christ, so the sin that was on you was placed on Jesus Christ instead. Also, the penalty you should have taken (being put to death) He took instead.

Therefore, Jesus was crucified on the cross. Your sins were placed on Him, and He died in your place. He died, was buried, and rose up on the third day having victory over death. Now He is in heaven interceding on your behalf all the time and ready to give you what you need out of agápe love to be able to have a love relationship with Him. Since your sin debt has been removed from you by the substitutionary death of Jesus, God looks upon you now as if you had never sinned. Your sin is removed, and now He's given you the free gift of eternal life. You are no longer dead. You are not under God's wrath. Instead, there has been a beautiful exchange. Your sin was placed on Jesus, and He took your punishment. Now Jesus has taken His righteousness and placed it upon you. When God looks upon you now, you are no longer separated because the righteousness of Jesus Christ covers you, and you are now acceptable before your Holy God.

What love! Are you having a hard time right now as you read this? Are you having a hard time accepting this love of Jesus? You may be saying, "I was raped. I was abused. I was abandoned. So many things happened to me. How can you say He loves me?" Let me say this to you, and I pray you will receive it. It was not the love of God that let you down. It was human love that failed you. Someone, out of selfishness and putting their needs above yours, did some act against you. They failed in their love. It was their love that should be rejected, not God's.

In the beginning of time, God never intended for such things to happen to you and to cause such harm. God created you and all mankind with a free will. You are not a robot. He will not make you love Him. You have a choice. Sometimes because you are in a sinful world and are around sinful people, you see how we may hurt each other. People may fail you and do evil things to you sometimes. They may talk about you, they may hurt you, abuse you, or rape you. Whether you are a Christian woman or not does not mean you will not get raped. Is it God that is doing it, or sinful man with his choices? Many traumatic events take place that only God understands (Deut. 29:29). Even then, God and His love will be there if you call out to Him. He will be there to sustain you and pick you up through rape, adultery, and everything else. You will see His agápe love is more than sufficient for you.

Dropped but Not Broken

Do you feel God is mad with you? Do you go on with a cloud of guilt or shame hovering over you? Do you feel alone and believe everyone else is doing so well? Do you want to run away? Do you feel you cannot trust God or believe what He says in His Word? Do you have no interest in studying His Word, or do you find yourself doing everything else before making time to be in His Word? Do you feel left out or have feelings of insecurity? Are you considering some major decision you know moves you further away from God? Has something happened in your life that makes it hard to believe God cares, much less loves you? Have you tried to live faithfully, but nothing seems to be going right?

Are you rejecting His love even now? Have you put your fist up at Him when really He has not failed you? It is the human love that failed you. You live in a fallen world, and you are among fallen people, and you, along with them, make choices that are just not godly and not according to this agápe love. That person treated you that way because they were not functioning in His agápe love. The only person that is able to function in this love is the person that has received Jesus Christ as his or her Lord and Savior. It is when you realize that you have sinned. It is when you repent (that means to have a change of mind and heart and go in a new direction). It is when you call out to God and say something to the effect, "I've been going the wrong way; I've been mad at you. I have been rejecting your love, because all the time I looked at You as the villain. I realize now it is the human love that has failed me, not You. I have been accusatory of You, but now I see the truth. God, I am open to your love. I am willing to be vulnerable and submit myself to You. I want Your agápe love flowing from the inside out. I want the ability to be able to *receive* Your love and to *give* it to others."

If you have never prayed this prayer before, please pray it now. If you do, you will *receive* God's beloved son Jesus Christ, who died in your place and who has already made provision for you to experience His agápe love. Pray believing Jesus died in your place, He was crucified, buried, and rose again the third day. He has taken your sin debt and placed it on the cross, and now He is able to place His robe of righteousness on you so you can be reconciled to a holy God who wants to have a love relationship with you. Pray this prayer believing in your heart, and saying it with your mouth, and you will be saved (Rom. 10:9–10). You will have God's Spirit come into you and give you the capacity to love:

to love the unlovable, to love someone of a different denomination, to love a Democrat, to love a Republican, to love someone who gets on your nerves, to love someone who stinks, etc. God's love will give you the capacity to love in ways you cannot even begin to understand! It will be a new way of life for you!

So pray this prayer with your mouth now as instructed by Romans 10:9–10 (NIV):

Lord Jesus, I acknowledge that I have sinned. I acknowledge you took my sin upon you and paid my sin debt that I could not pay. You died in my place and took the punishment that I deserved. Forgive me of my sin and give me your free gift of eternal life. Come into my life and be my Savior and Lord. Please place your robe of righteousness upon me and restore me into a right relationship with God the Father that I may walk in sincere agápe love. Thank you for saving me and making me your child. In Jesus's Name, Amen.

Praise God! Hallelujah! If you have prayed that prayer for the first time, all of heaven is rejoicing over you right now. First John 5:12 (KJV) says, *"He that has the Son has life, and he that does not have the Son of God does not have life."* Since you prayed today putting your faith in what Jesus did for you, you have received Jesus Christ, God's Son. That means you have eternal life. At the moment you take your last breath, you will depart and be with God in Heaven. You will not perish by going to Hell and eternal separation. If you have chosen not to accept Jesus Christ, you do not have eternal life. Read the Scripture again in 1 John. If you have the Son, you have life (eternal life). If you do not have the Son, you do not have life (eternal life).

Now that you have received God's Son, Jesus Christ, you not only have eternal life, but, according to the Scripture you just read, God's Holy Spirit will be in you. He will give you the capacity to agápe love even those who set themselves up to be your enemy.

Another thing that is important for you to know is that nothing will ever be able to separate you from God's love. Nothing! There are many things that can cause a separation in human relationships, but nothing will ever separate you from the love of God now that you have accepted His Son (Rom. 8:35–39). God loves you so much that first of all, He sent His Son Jesus Christ to die just for you. Then, what God did was write a whole big love letter to you—the Bible. In the Bible, He expresses and tells you how much He loves you. So not only did He send His begotten Son to pay your sin debt and to take your wrath upon Him, but He also tells you all about it and writes a love letter containing more details in His Holy Word (Bible). The more you read the Bible, the more you will understand this sincere agápe love.

What you have just read is the Gospel message of Jesus Christ. It is a message of salvation—saving all who believe it. It is how a person becomes a child of God or is born again spiritually. It is indeed a "one size fits all" message for all who will decide His Words are true. If you have just prayed this prayer of faith, you have received God's agápe love. Now you will learn to give this same agápe love to others. Not sure that you can? Oh yes, you can!

Yes, You Can

Amanda's nephew, Carl, was the most obnoxious child she had ever known. She did not love him or even want to be around him. There was nine years between him and his older sibling, who was a girl. His father was so glad to have a boy child that he refused to discipline him. Things got worse when he became a teenager. He went to college and majored in music and became a fine musician, but he lived the life of a hippie. Amanda did not spend much time in prayer over him, but now realizes how good God is for not giving up on any of us. Hebrews 7:25 lets us know how even Jesus intercedes and prays for us.

Amanda's sister, Carl's mother, died of breast cancer at the young age of sixty. Two years previously, the father had died of a rare brain disease. Carl got married and moved to California. Then Carl started to send Amanda gifts and letters. He would even pick up the phone and call her to let her know how much he loved her. Amanda began to respond in like manner. Today Carl is sixty-six years old and has become a very loving person who is sensitive to others. He is a kind and good husband and father. Amanda learned a lot about God's love through her experience with Carl. She saw how God's love is never ending. She truly loves Carl now but regrets not loving him and praying for him when he needed it the most. She sees clearly today how faithful God is in spite of our actions.

In the section "No Substitute for Love" we saw the contrast between our love and that of God's unconditional loyal love. Like Amanda, we can put conditions on our relationships and on whether we will love others or not. God is love and cannot cease to be the very essence of love. In the next section we will discuss more relational challenges. For now, praise God for His love not being based on what you do. The

Dropped but Not Broken

more you understand and receive His love, the more it will provide unshakeable ground for you to build other love relationships upon.

You can be confident in your quest for opening your heart to receive and give love once again. Receive God's love first, and then you will be able to give love to another. If you reverse the order, you will be defeated. In other words, there will be no fulfilled love walk without God as your internal source. When the deep desire for love is quenched within you, love will overflow to others around you.

Mark 3:14 (KJV) states, *"And he ordained twelve, that they should be with him, and that he might send them forth to preach."* The twelve apostles had to spend time with Jesus first and be ministered to before they could leave to minister to others. This is true of you as well. Yes, you can love the worst person, but not out of your own resources. This is one of the keys to let you know whether you are saved—you love others with the love of God. If you love others with the love of God, it is a proof God is in you, since God is love.

Remember what it says in 2 Corinthians 3:5–6 (NLT), *"It is not that we think we are qualified to do anything on our own. Our qualification comes from God. He has enabled us to be ministers of his new covenant."* On your own you cannot love correctly, but God will qualify and enable you to carry out His will. You will have many opportunities to love the unlovable, but you do not have to fret. God is the one who will help you do so. It is at those times you must remember He has qualified and enabled you to love another person regardless of his or her actions.

Romans 5:5 lets you know that the love of God has been poured into your heart. You received the Holy Spirit when you prayed to receive Jesus Christ as your Savior. The love of God is poured into your heart by Him. You have the capacity to love in a way you have never been able to love before. Romans 8:37 says you are more than a conqueror through Him who loves you. You are able to love because God first loved you (1 John 4:19). Philippians 4:13 (NLT) states, *"For I can do everything through Christ, who gives me strength."*

Philippians 2:13 (NLT) states, *"For God is working in you, giving you the desire and the power to do what pleases him."* Who is doing the work—you or God? This passage is such a comfort. It lets you know God is the one who is working in you to want to do what is right. Then He will work on your behalf to give you the power to carry it out. He will not fail you in this love walk. It is you who will have to neglect Him for it not to be carried out.

Also, 2 Corinthians 1:9–10 (NKJV) states, *"Yes, we had the sentence of death in ourselves, that we should not trust in ourselves but in God who raises the dead, who delivered us from so great a death, and does deliver us; in whom we trust that He will still deliver us."* This is another passage that brings such consolation. It shows you have been delivered (past), He is delivering now (present), and He will still deliver you in the future (future). God is faithful to you, even when you do not recognize it. This passage deals with the past, the present, and the future. What is left out? You have already been delivered from death (eternal death and separation from God) if you have prayed that prayer of faith by the love of God. You are now being delivered on a daily basis by the love of God. You will be delivered in the future from the very presence of sin by the love of God when Jesus Christ returns. You cannot lose if you will just believe in what God has said and live it out in your life!

In this section, "Loyal Love," it would be good to review some of what was discussed. Those involved in the Godhead have always had a love relationship before the world began. Giving and receiving love is just a part of their nature. In fact, God is love, and there is no agápe love apart from Him. God does not just give love—**He is love**.

You understand by now you have two deep-down desires that are given to you by God. A need to *receive* love—we want to be loved. Also, you have a need to *give* love to others. These are the two desires that were given to you by God. They are also the fulfillment of His command in Matthew 22:37–40 (NLT) that states, *"Jesus replied, 'You must love the Lord your God with all your heart, all your soul, and all your mind.' This is the first and greatest commandment. A second is equally important: 'Love your neighbor as yourself.' The entire law and all the demands of the prophets are based on these two commandments."*

Dropped but Not Broken

Remember the illustration of the cross? Remember the vertical piece of wood representing Jesus and the horizontal piece of wood representing all other relationships? In this section of the book, the vertical part of *receiving* love was discussed. We will discuss the horizontal part of *giving* in the next section of the book. Jesus, God's Son, is the One who was sent down here so we would be able to be reconciled back to God and to be able to receive all of His love and all that His love has to give: all of His grace, all of His empowerment through His Spirit, and all of the ability needed to love God and others each day. The psalmist said in Psalm 46:1 (KJV), *"God is our refuge and strength, a very present help in trouble."*

I shared with you "God is love." If you want your need to receive love fulfilled, it can only be fulfilled in God. God is where that source of love comes from. He always wants to lavish His love upon you. When you decide to put anything else before His love, the love you replace His with is going to come up empty. It will come to nothing. There are no substitutes for His love. You need to receive God's love and let God's love flow into these other relationships. The other relationships are not wrong. They are His instruments to love you all the more.

The other thing, too, is God's love is always being expressed to you in action and in sacrifice. He really does not have to do so. But eternally He has a loyal love for you. Zephaniah 3:17 (NIV) says, *"The Lord your God is with you, he is mighty to save. He will take great delight in you, he will quiet you with his love, he will rejoice over you with singing."* Do you picture God rejoicing over you and singing?

Second Samuel 22:17–20 (NLT) says, *"He reached down from heaven and rescued me; he drew me out of deep waters. He rescued me from my powerful enemies, from those who hated me and were too strong for me. They attacked me at a moment when I was in distress, but the Lord supported me. He led me to a place of safety; he rescued me because he delights in me."*

Psalm 34:17–18 (NKJV) says, *"The righteous cry out and the Lord hears and delivers them out of all of their troubles. The Lord is near to those who have a broken heart and such as have a contrite spirit* (or broken spirit)." Jesus is able to help us to receive His sincere agápe love. What you are going to learn as you continue to read is how to give that love back to God and to others.

John 15:9 (NKJV) says, *"As the Father loved me, I also have loved you, abide in my love."* So abide, continue, and remain in the love of God and do not let other things or other people take the place of God's love. There is no substitute for His love. Cast aside all fears and doubt, for, yes, you can open your heart again to love!

Be mindful that if you try to work for God's love and approval it will only lead to rejection. You will be living in opposition to the completed work of Jesus Christ on the cross. This is living like the religious leaders who were proud of keeping rules and regulations. The sad thing is they were relying on their own works and rejecting the finished work of Christ on their behalf. This, of course, is not acceptable to God at all. The only way to please the Father is through His Son. All His Son did was for the purpose of bringing us to God. There was nothing we could do on our own to make us acceptable before God. When you rely on what you do to be pleasing to God, you are no different. You have made the work of Jesus Christ void in your life. You can tell if this is happening when you live day in and day out with guilt and shame. The reason the guilt and shame are dominant is because your focus is on what you are doing and not on what Christ has done to cleanse you from all sin, guilt, and shame. If you are still under a cloud of condemnation and judgment, reread the section "One Size Fits All" and pray the prayer of faith so you can be forgiven of all of your sins. Then the work of Jesus on the cross will be applied to your life, and you will be able to live in peace and freedom.

Dropped but Not Broken

It is going to take relentless dependence upon the Lord to live in this manner. Some feel success is never making a mistake or failing or stumbling in life. This cannot be further from the truth. It is through your trials, weaknesses, and failures that you learn to rely on God and see Him move on your behalf. In yourself you cannot love at all. If you will let Him show you how to love and even supply the very love you need personally and will give to others, your journey on this love walk will be blessed. You will have to take one step at a time, leaning on Jesus all the way. Cease from your own works and rely upon Jesus working in and through you. He will allow you to experience many ups and downs, but you will learn more about His love and your capacity to sincerely love as a result.

Basically, God is saying, "Just surrender to Me. *I am love.* I have all the supply of love you need. If you want to be able to give love, just yield to Me. You don't have to have some special knowledge, and you do not have to accomplish some special work. If you will just come to Me and be an empty vessel, I will fill you with My love, and I will work it out in your life. I will show you what this love can do. I will show you how this love can operate for you even when you do not want it to. Just empty yourself of all other preconceived notions of how you can take steps to be more loving. Lay aside what you saw on the television or what you read in that magazine, and believe My Words to you. You will not understand how you are able to deal with people in a totally different way than before."

Continue on your journey to the next part of this book on "Love Lens" that you may see more clearly what this love looks like when it is functioning in your life. Concerned that you cannot? Oh yes, you can. Let 1 Thessalonians 5:23–24 (NLT) remind you who is doing the work and who will complete the work in you.

"Now may the God of peace make you holy in every way, and may your whole spirit and soul and body be kept blameless until our Lord Jesus Christ comes again. God will make this happen, for he who calls you is faithful."

Smile; Jesus loves you!

Part 3

Love Lens
"The Horizontal Solution"

Part 3:
Love Lens – "The Horizontal Solution"

"You were cleansed from your sins when you obeyed the truth, so now you must show sincere love to each other as brothers and sisters. Love each other deeply with all your heart."

(1 Pet. 1:22, NLT).

Having covered the vertical part of our cross illustration in reference to our *receiving* love and our relationship with Jesus, now we will concentrate on *giving* love and the horizontal relationships (spouse, friends, and family) that are encountered in one's life. In actuality, we are blessed when we are both "receiving and giving" in both directions illustrated by the cross. Consequently, we both receive and should give love back to God (vertical); and we should give love whether it is received or not (horizontal). To the world this is foolishness and bondage, but to God it is wisdom and your pathway to freedom.

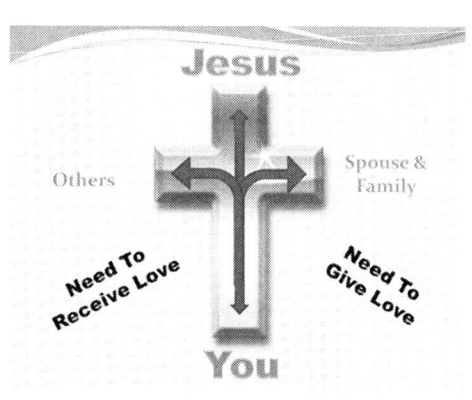

You cannot give what you do not have, so having received God's love you can now extend it to others—love from the inside out. He will always be the source and power of your love. Without Him you do not have the power to love in an unconditional and sacrificial way. He desires for you to become the channel whereby His love passes to others. The power from the first relationship will always provide for the others. Intimate relationships always have some risk involved. There is vulnerability and a chance to be hurt or misunderstood. He provides wisdom and security for us as we relate to others, since Christians live by faith (2 Cor. 5:7).

Also, it is important to know what is meant by putting your relationship with Christ first. It does not mean you avoid relationships with others until you get everything in place with the Lord. This would be impossible, for you interact with others all the time. Truly the sanctifying process discussed earlier is going to continue until you go to Heaven to be with the Lord. So you will never have it all together while living here on earth. Yet, there is a way to put the Lord first while interacting with others at the same time. This will be covered more in depth in Part 4 "Love Light." Now let's concentrate on your love lens.

A lens is made out of a piece of glass or plastic shaped to focus or spread light rays that pass through it for the purpose of forming an image. First John 1:5 (KJV) states, *"This then is the message which we have heard of him, and declare unto you, that God is light, and in him is no darkness at all."* So in this section continue your journey and allow the light of God to pass through your mind and heart to form a clear image of what His love is and how it operates in your life. In other words, what does His love look like?

What Does Love Look Like?

Cheryl's husband died in October. Those months following his death were filled not only with grief but also with mind-boggling business problems. Although Tony had a serious heart condition (complicated by mouth cancer and debilitating cobalt treatments), she was lulled into thinking he had conquered it. The heart problem appeared to be stabilized by medication and diet, and the tumor had shrunk beyond detection. So his death was a shock. Family and friends rallied around for a longer than usually anticipated period of time, supporting her through horrendous problems. Finally these were resolved, and she turned toward "getting on with her life."

Fortunately, she had completed her master's degree two years before Tony's death, so she was in a better position to return to her profession in human services (having resigned to assist him with his business). Being immersed in a rewarding job led her to increasing independence. Her church responsibilities and activities in single Christian groups were fulfilling too. Her three married children lived in other states, but there were regular visits to them, and they visited her. She frequently threw her suitcase in her car on a Friday morning and left her office that afternoon for Washington, DC, or Connecticut for a weekend visit with her son or daughter. There were also annual visits to San Francisco to visit another son. She kept active and positive, and she was blessed with good health. Yet, "something was missing." She was trying to live with an inner void.

The cover story in the March 1984 issue of *Guideposts* was written by Marjorie Holmes. Cheryl read Marjorie's books, and her thoughts, her feelings, and her writings helped to sustain Cheryl. She felt as though Marjorie knew her—that they were friends. And what a delightful article she wrote about falling in love with George. It gave Cheryl a wonderful feeling of happiness for them both. However, Cheryl had to admit she missed "a close companionship—"someone special." So, she began to pray, "Please, God, send me a wonderful man who will love me and who I can love." She was not in a hurry. She felt if it was God's will, it would happen. She was ready to accept widowhood for the rest of her life if He deemed it. She would continue her involvement with the single Christians' groups.

However, one year after she began this supplication, she met Stanley, who was a widower too. They both were involved in an organization together. They were immediately attracted to each other. She felt it was love at first sight. She ceased praying for someone; somehow she knew it was Stanley. They were soon married, and the support from their children on both sides warmed her heart. It was a small, beautiful candlelight ceremony in her old church with only their families present. She lay in the bed one night thanking God for Stanley and wondering how she could ever deserve him. It seemed a heavenly voice clearly replied, "But you prayed for him." For sure, God had answered her prayer!

It has already been established that God is love. If you want to know what love looks like, you must see God. The beautiful thing is, God has not hidden Himself from you. The opposite is true. He has gone overboard to reveal Himself to you so you may see Him and know His love. What does love look like? It looks like God.

Of course, the love of God operates in a multitude of circumstances in various ways. So we are really taking a glimpse right now. Hopefully, this will get you to be more sensitive in recognizing His love as you live your life each day—whether you see His love operating through you or through others.

Looking at 1 John 4:7–8 (NLT), it reads, *"Dear friends, let us continue to love one another, for love comes from God. Anyone who loves is a child of God and knows God. But anyone who does not love does not know God, for God is love."* This passage confirms love is not a human achievement but divine in its origin. As a child of God, you are capable of love. For His divine power of love is provided to His children. If you are not a child of God, you will not be able to operate in agápe love. You can love from an earthly perspective (eros, storge, and phileo), but it will not be in the sincere agápe love of God. So when love is in operation, you are actually seeing God being manifested.

First John 4:9–15 (NLT) says, *"God showed how much he loved us by sending his one and only Son into the world so that we might have eternal life through him. This is real love—not that we loved God, but that he loved us and sent his Son as a sacrifice to take away our sins. Dear friends, since God loved us that much, we surely ought to love each other. No one has ever seen God. But if we love each other, God lives in us, and his love is brought to full expression in us. And God has given us his Spirit as proof that we live in him and he in us. Furthermore, we have seen with our own eyes and now testify that the Father sent his Son to be the Savior of the world. All who confess that Jesus is the Son of God have God living in them, and they live in God."* Look at what this is saying; if you want to see real love, you do not look at how you love God but at how He loves you. So to understand what love looks like, your focus should always be on God and how He expresses His love. As you learn more and more how to love, remember to praise God for operating through you, for this love does not originate from you. You cannot take credit for sincerely loving another.

When love is operating in you, you will always see love expressed through action and not just words. The action is usually sacrificial. This is how you can recognize this love. It does not seek its own; it is not selfish. To make sure you could see exactly what sacrificial love looks like, God demonstrated it by the sacrificial death of His Beloved Son. God your Father loves the Son in a way you cannot understand here on earth. Any good parent hurts when their child is hurt. Likewise, when you give up something very precious to you to another who does not deserve it at all, you are seeing this love in operation. As God, you will love not because a person is worthy of it, but you love because it is your (God's) very nature to do so.

I trust you are reading these passages slowing and truly digesting what they are saying. It will be life-changing for you. Look at what 1 John 4:16 (NLT) says, *"We know how much God loves us, and we have put our trust in his love. God is love, and all who live in love live in God, and God lives in them."* Love and faith are intertwined. Faith is having absolute trust and confidence in God regardless of the circumstance or consequences. Look at how faith is expressed in this passage: (1) we know, (2) put our trust, (3) God is, (4) live in God, and (5) God lives in them. You can see God's love in you when you stand by faith against all odds and all opposition because [in reference to numbers above]: (1) you know God loves you and is working in a way you may not understand right now; (2) you have made a decision you are going to trust Him and not be controlled by what you see or feel; (3) you know that God is—He is superior over all things (sovereign, almighty, protector, provider, deliverer, etc.); and (4 and 5) you are in God and He lives in you. By faith you know greater is He that is in you than he (Satan) who is in the world. I cannot recall the source, but I had read once: "No closer relationship is possible than for a person to abide in God and to have God abiding in him. It is hard for us to visualize such a relationship, but we might compare it, in the natural realm, to a poker in the fire, a sponge in the water, or a balloon in the air. In each case, the object is in an element and the element is in the object." God in you, and you in God—this is what love looks like.

We can continue to see love in 1 John 4:17–18 (NLT), which says, *"And as we live in God, our love grows more perfect. So we will not be afraid on the day of judgment, but we can face him with confidence because we live like Jesus here in this world. Such love has no fear, because perfect love expels all fear. If we are afraid, it is for fear of punishment, and this shows that we have not fully experienced his perfect love."* As you surrender your selfish ways to God and let His unconditional love flow through you, you will be living like Jesus here in this world. God manifested Himself to the world through the life of His Son. Since Jesus has returned to the Father in Heaven, you will be the one to manifest Him to the world. God is made known to the world through love. You know a person is a Christian by agápe love. If a person lives in fear all the time (especially of dying and facing God) and does not display love, the passage says this shows that person has not fully experienced God's perfect love. God's perfect love is given in salvation through His Son. As you live in God your love will grow and be perfected. As you continue to love as Jesus, you will not have to be fearful or ashamed on the Day of Judgment, for you will be facing the One who loves you and who you love in return. Christians are not judged in regards to their eternal destiny but in regards to what rewards they will or will not receive (John 5:24, 1 Cor. 3:12–15, and 2 Cor. 5:10). Since you are living a life of love, you have nothing to fear when you face God. The Bible Knowledge Commentary reads:

> *The word fear has to do with punishment or literally, "fear has punishment." Fear carries with it a kind of torment that is its own punishment. Ironically, an unloving believer experiences punishment precisely because he feels guilty and is afraid to meet his Judge. Such fear prohibits a completed love (one who fears is not made perfect in love). But a Christian who loves has nothing to fear and thus escapes the inner torment which a failure to love can bring.*

First John 4:19–21 (NLT) states, *"We love each other because he loved us first. If someone says, 'I love God,' but hates a Christian brother or sister, that person is a liar; for if we don't love people we can see, how can we love God, whom we cannot see? And he has given us this command: Those who love God must also love their Christian brothers and sisters."* You love another brother or sister in Christ because God first loved you. Even though Christians have the capacity to love as Jesus did on the earth, it does not mean that all will humbly do so. It is hypocritical to say you love God and hate a Christian brother or sister. As Christians we are called to live a life of love and be different from unbelievers in the world. Why would unbelievers want salvation in Christ if it does not make a difference in the lives of those who call themselves Christians? Christians are called to love unbelievers too, but we are commanded to start with other believers as a testimony to God's love in the world. This passage calls a person a liar if they say they love God and yet hate another Christian. Love and hate are not mutual. So God's love is seen when Christians display love one for another.

Another passage of Scripture that lets us know what love looks like is Galatians 5:22–23, where the fruit of the Spirit is listed. These virtues listed are divinely produced by God's indwelling Spirit (fruit of the Spirit) and can never be produced by human effort. Note "fruit" is singular and not plural. The fruit of the Spirit is love. Love, listed first, is the umbrella over which, or basis upon which, the other virtues operate. They do not function apart from love. Really this fruit is the life of Christ lived out in a believer. There is so much more that can be said of the fruit, but I will condense my comments to what love looks like when operating in your life.

So here are some additional ways in which you can see what love looks like.

Galatians 5:22–23 (NLT)—*But the Holy Spirit produces this kind of fruit in our lives:*

The first three are in relation to God:

> *Love*—what God is; self-sacrificing
>
> *Joy*—contentment and satisfaction with God and with what He allows
>
> *Peace*—harmonious relationship with God that overflows to others

The next three are in relation to others:

> *Patience*—(long-suffering) self-restraint and long endurance when offended
>
> *Kindness*—an unselfish spirit of doing for others; benevolence
>
> *Goodness*—doing to others even when it is not deserved

And the last three are in relation to one's own inner life:

> *Faithfulness*—being trustworthy and reliable
>
> *Gentleness*—considerate of others
>
> *Self-Control*—to restrain fleshly impulses

There is no law against these things! As you live under the control of the Spirit, He will produce these Christlike characteristics in you.

As you live and abide in Christ, there is no need for a law to demand right behavior or to control you. For His Holy Spirit will instruct and convict and be in control of you, spewing forth the righteousness of Christ through your life.

Colossians 3:12–14 (NLT) reveals further what love looks like: *Since God chose you to be the holy people he loves, you must clothe yourselves with:*

> *Tenderhearted Mercy*—a heart of compassion
>
> *Kindness*—an unselfish spirit of doing for others
>
> *Humility*—absence of pride; ability to esteem others better than yourself
>
> *Gentleness*—(meekness) does not mean weakness, but strength under control
>
> *Patience*—self-restraint and long endurance when offended

Make allowance for each other's faults, and forgive anyone who offends you. Remember, the Lord forgave you, so you must forgive others. Above all, clothe yourselves with love, which binds us all together in perfect harmony.

Likewise in this passage, love holds everything together in perfect unity. Are you getting a picture of what this love looks like? Also, as you look at the lists, are you seeing why they cannot be done in your own strength?

All right, one more list to review. This is the most popular list people refer to when trying to see what love looks like in a person's life. Do not feel overwhelmed by these lists. You know you cannot produce any of these virtues in your life, but He *can* and *will* if you will submit to His control in your life. Whew! Doesn't that make you feel better? I would suggest you prayerfully go over these lists and ask the Lord to produce His love in you. Pray specifically and in faith, anticipating the Holy Spirit to produce this fruit in your life.

Let's look at 1 Corinthians 13:1–8 (NKJV), *Though I speak with the tongues of men and of angels, but have not love, I have become sounding brass or a clanging cymbal. And though I have the gift of prophecy, and understand all mysteries and all knowledge, and though I have all faith, so that I could remove mountains, but have not love, I am nothing. And though I bestow all my goods to feed the poor, and though I give my body to be burned, but have not love, it profits me nothing.*

> *Love suffers long and is kind*—patient endurance; actively good to others

Love does not envy—pleased when others are honored or exalted

Love does not parade itself, is not puffed up—avoids pride; does not sing one's own praises

Does not behave rudely, does not seek its own, is not provoked, thinks no evil—considerate; not suspicious or selfish; does not keep track of others' offenses

Does not rejoice in iniquity, but rejoices in the truth—no pleasure in unrighteous acts or another's downfall

Bears all things, believes all things, hopes all things, endures all things—remains steadfast in difficulties; believes the best of another unless convinced otherwise; hopeful instead of critical; positive instead of negative

Love never fails.

There will never be an end to love (God has no beginning or end). For all eternity love will exist (1 Cor. 13:13). You may ask, "Then why are so many relationships failing?" The answer more than likely is that many are operating in a love that is an imitation of the real thing; it is a makeshift that cannot endure. Yet, I have seen those who grasp hold of God's love for them personally; then they allow Him to love others through them, and then miraculously their lives change. When they do so, their relationships are strong, alive, and endure. You have reached this point in the book. Good for you! You evidently are serious about a love walk. What path will you pursue in your relationships? Will you choose agápe love or will you choose to love in word and tongue?

In Word or Tongue

Jantz was beginning to doubt Jeff's love, for he always said the right thing but never followed through with any action. His words were tantalizing to her, but he never showed the love he so eloquently expressed. The Bible has wisdom that Jantz could use. First John 3:18 (NIV) says, *"Dear children, let us not love with words or tongue but with actions and in truth."* This is addressed to "Dear children." The "Dear children" are Christians, God's beloved children. It is letting you know the test of true love is not one's verbal profession of it (loving with words or tongue), but in a willingness to love with actions and in truth. To love *with words* is to feel love and speak loving words but stop short of doing anything. To love in *tongue* is to profess or express what is not true. An example is a guy who says he loves you but does not mean it. The opposite of loving with words is to love in deed, and the opposite of loving in tongue is to love in truth. An example of this is a guy who genuinely puts his love into action concerning you, and he speaks the truth from his heart. He does not defraud you by just telling you what you want to hear or by telling you deceitful lies.

    God told us he loved us, but He also put His words into action. Love is a verb; it is always expressed in action. We should do the same. Do not settle for a guy whose love is just "word and tongue." Even if someone is unlearned or shy in showing his love, there ought to be a willingness to learn and put God's Word into action. Another thing that is important is to not be controlling in this area, but to learn to appreciate and accept how your mate may try to express his love for you. Do not squash his efforts by belittling him. It may cause him to give up and not want to try again. And by all means, do not be the one who loves a man only with words and tongue. If you do not want to have someone defraud you, then don't defraud another yourself.

If you are a young lady reading this book, and you think there is a "soul mate" for you out there, please know this is a lie from the pit that will keep you in bondage. Your "soul mate" is Jesus Christ. Only he can touch your soul and keep you. I pray you are not one who is desperately trying to figure out and find the "one" who belongs to you. This type of thinking leads to all forms of sin and deceit. Right now you have Jesus, and He has promised to not withhold any good thing from you if you will walk (live) upright (Ps. 84:11). You may have a dream, but He knows if the fulfillment of your dream will only lead to heartache. In faith, trust Him with your needs.

If you are a married woman reading this book, maybe you are asking, "Did I marry the right person?" Why are you even entertaining such a question? You are married. Love the person you are with; by giving him agápe love, you may see it return to you. If it is a true desire of your heart, Jesus will enable you to agápe your spouse. Just be careful as to any lustful thoughts you may entertain about other men. Now, I understand some women reading this book may be in an abusive situation or in a marriage with someone who pretended to be a Christian and is living like the devil's right-hand man. Possibly this has caused you to question your relationship. This is quite understandable, and you may have to be separated from him for your own safety. I was talking about a woman who has a good man (who is not perfect) but who is still questioning and wondering if there could be someone better suited for her out there. This is a form of doubt that can open the door for all kinds of evil mischief. If you are under this attack, stop right now, put the book down, and ask God to deliver you from such thoughts. Ask Him to help you agápe your husband and respect him although he has flaws. Pray and ask God to get the log out of your own eyes and then you will be able to see your husband much better through the eyes of Jesus (Matt. 7:5).

When you go on a date with someone who doesn't know Jesus, can he really love you? No. Why? For the very reason that God is love. Therefore, when you go on a date, and this guy says, "You know, if you love me, you will prove it." Or, "You should show me at least this one time." Listen to me; please let me have your attention. When you hear that, pick your pocketbook up as quick as you can and run as far away from him as your feet will carry you! He is lusting after you. He is not operating in God's love toward you. Agápe love is not selfish. It always looks out for what is best for the other person. However, lust is selfish and is always looking out for its own needs. He is operating in tongue … beware! Remember, outside of the realm of marriage, whenever you are being asked to give your body for love, it's not love at all, but lust. Second Corinthians 6:14 instructs you not to be unequally yoked with a nonbeliever. This has to do with a woman who is not married presently and has a choice in who she marries. If you have your eyes on someone who has rejected Christ, you need to reject the notion of getting involved with him. To do otherwise is deliberate disobedience. Let go of any thoughts of evangelistic dating. Do not presume upon God's grace.

If you are already married to a nonbeliever, then 1 Corinthians 7:27 instructs you not to seek to be separated from him. First Peter 3:1–6 also gives instruction for a wife in this situation. Depending on the type of man he is, it may take more grace for you to love in the way instructed. God is able to give you what is needed to love your husband in spite of his being a nonbeliever. As a matter of fact, your behavior expressed through love could be the very thing used of God to bring him to a saving knowledge of Jesus. Get with a Christian counselor if you need more help in this area. Also, go to our website for additional help.

You saw in the Word that you can tell whether you are a Christian by the love of God operating in and through you. God's Spirit is placed in us when we receive Jesus Christ as our Lord and Savior. Along with the Spirit comes spiritual fruit. The foundation of this fruit is love. As a Christian, you will be learning about this love until Christ returns. You never get to a point where you have arrived and need not grow any further. You will always be challenged as to whether your love will be with actions and in truth.

What if your parents never taught you how to love? What if they were divorced? What if you were hurt by someone who said they loved you? Do you still have the capacity to love? If you have received God as your Savior, you do have the capacity to love. God is in you. It doesn't matter. You can start today. If you think your capacity to love is zero, you can start today by understanding and receiving God's love and being able to walk it out one step at a time. It is good if you have parents that can give an example of agápe love, but they are not the source of agápe love. And yes, they can demonstrate it, but they are not the ones to distribute it to you. It is God alone who can do so.

First Corinthians 13:1–3 (NKJV) states, *"Though I speak with the tongues of men and of angels, but have not love, I have become sounding brass or a clanging cymbal. And though I have the gift of prophecy, and understand all mysteries and all knowledge, and though I have all faith, so that I could remove mountains, but have not love, I am nothing. And though I bestow all my goods to feed the poor, and though I give my body to be burned, but have not love, it profits me nothing."*

Take hold of what can be concluded from this passage. Any other love relationship that does not include this agápe love amounts to nothing. It equals zero. It is not going to constantly fulfill your needs. What you don't want to happen to you is to try to get your love tank filled with only that which is produced by humans at the neglect of God's love. Try not to forget that Jesus is able to fill your love tank just like that. All of the other relationships are additional blessings.

"O How I Love Jesus" is an old song with this chorus, *"Oh, how I love Jesus, because He first loved me."* Love did not begin with you. You did not initiate it. God took action and operated in truth so you may know how much He loves you. The steadfast love of the Lord never ceases (Lam. 3:22). His love is unfailing and exceeds our wildest imagination—from salvation to glory and from birth to death. His love is always expressed with actions and in truth. Likewise, your love is expressed in action and in truth when you do not erect loved ones as idols.

Loved Ones as Idols

Delores was in her forties before she was married to Bruce. Now that she had him, she did everything in her power to keep him happy. The one thing that became a growing problem was that Bruce was putting more time into his business than he was in his relationship with the Lord. He worked so hard during the week he always wanted to get away or rest on the weekends. He enjoyed spending quiet time with Delores. He truly loved her but seemed to have less and less time for developing his love for Jesus. Now Delores, seldom attending church and being less involved than she was before marriage, has noticed she too was finding less time to even read her Bible and pray.

Jeremiah 2:11–13 (NLT) says, *"Has any nation ever traded its gods for new ones, even though they are not gods at all? Yet my people have exchanged their glorious God for worthless idols! The heavens are shocked at such a thing and shrink back in horror and dismay," says the Lord. "For my people have done two evil things: They have abandoned me—the fountain of living water. And they have dug for themselves cracked cisterns that can hold no water at all!"*

There are so many scenarios that play out in daily situations whereby others, not just loved ones, may take preeminence over God's will for you. Most people think of idols from the Old Testament, but whenever our desire is to please another more than God, that individual has become an idol. Satan is very subtle in slipping us into a mind-set where we become dependent on another individual more than on God. Sometimes you do not even realize it is taking place. Yet, this is one way you can recognize it. Whenever you stress over knowing what another person says or thinks, in addition to the Word of God, you are on slippery ground. This does not mean God cannot confirm His Word through others. Yet, if you are dependent upon another's opinion in addition to or above the Lord's, you are in trouble. It does not matter who it is (pastor, best friend, etc.). You have erected an idol over Jesus. Another way to tell if your feet are sliding is when you do not want to be rejected by the individual(s) if you obey the Lord. Your concern for them is more important than your concern for obeying God. You dread the possibility of losing them or not pleasing them. John 12:43 (NKJV) says, *"For they loved the praise of men more than the praise of God."* Revelation 2:4 (NKJV) says, *"Nevertheless I have this against you, that you have left your first love."*

Ann grew up in a close-knit family. They would always look out for one another and take care of each other. Ann's brother, Gregory, was an accountant at a large company. One day he confided to Ann that he was swindling money from his company. Now he was involving Ann and promising that once he was back on his feet, he would return the money. So Ann began to help Gregory in his evil schemes.

Patricia never thought she would end up marrying a pastor, but Luther swept her off her feet. He was charming and seemed to know the Bible inside and out. Nevertheless, her suspicions were confirmed when she stepped into the church office unexpectedly one night and saw Luther cover the pornography on his computer. Although she was devastated, she continued to cover up for him so others in the church would not know and be hurt by his actions.

Monica was a part of the singles' group and enjoyed the activities that were planned. Her sister, Sharon, was new to the group, but Monica was jealous of her. No one in the group knew it, but she carried bitterness in her heart toward Sharon. She was asked to lead the discussion on love one month but made an excuse for why she could not do it. Although she knew her attitude was not pleasing to the Lord, she would not relinquish her grudge against Sharon.

Beverly had determined she would not raise her children in the same way as her parents raised her. She made sure they had the best of everything. If she had to work overtime or take money out of her husband's wallet, she made sure they did not go without. Although she had wished her son and daughter would attend church with her, she stopped asking them. It appeared they would get upset and accuse her of pressuring them to do something they did not want to do.

Dropped but Not Broken

God is not against your having a spouse, family, or friends. He is the one who created these relationships. Please trust He knows the problems that can occur in relationships when His love is absent. Remember the love and unity among the Trinity? This is the very thing He desires for you in your other relationships as well. What He has established in relationships is for your good and not harm. The reason many women are being traumatized in relationships is because they have left God out of them.

There is an all-out war by Satan on the healthy relationships God has designed between spouses, family, and friends. Fantasy sexual partners, the lack of family time, cell phones, children running from one activity to another, a host of social media, overtime at work, etc. have eaten away at the fiber of strong relationships. For a couple to remain married, for children to make time with their parents, for family to be caretakers, for friends to consistently build each other up can be stressful and very demanding.

Life is all about relationships, but they can place demands upon our time, emotions, and energy. People are connected all the time by cell phones and social media, but these systems still seem to lack the deep emotional closeness that relationships once provided. People seem to have less time to build meaningful relationships. Everyone is in a hurry or stressed out. I heard the word "busy" can be used as an acrostic for "Being Under Satan's Yoke." That is so true, when we are constantly going and having no time for rest. We have fallen under the bondage of Satan. To change this trend, we need to slow down and stay connected to God and to others. Life is fleeting. No one will regret at the end of their lives the time well spent with close relationships.

Pulling some examples from the Scripture passages in the section "What Does Love Look Like," we will see how your other relationships can thrive when God's love is sustaining you and flowing through you. (You can refer back to that section if it helps.)

Galatians 5:22–23:

> **Patience**—*Audrey notices how God has provided her with patience in dealing with her teenager Ryan. He has become very defiant, and all she wants to do is lash back at him in*

> the same manner he has toward her. He knows just how to hurt her deeply. In her quiet time with the Lord, He revealed to her how constantly placing strict rules upon Ryan without developing a relationship with him has led to his rebellion. Rules without relationship lead to rebellion. God is giving her the grace and patience to know how to build and not tear down their relationship any further. She is not going to stop loving him because he is not what she wants him to be. She is thankful for how patient God has been with her through this trial. She is recognizing her temper tantrums and has purposed to not continue with this behavior. It is helping her to be patient with Ryan and allow him to grow as well.
>
> **Goodness**—Since Natalie's accident, she expects Susan to run at her beckon and call. Susan is married with four children, but Natalie expects her friend to do her grocery shopping and run her errands each week. Susan is able to extend goodness to Natalie because by the grace of God He has given her the needed strength for these extra tasks. Additionally, she knows it was only God who moved on her husband to give extra help with their children at this time without her asking. She is praising Him for intervening in her life and making a way out of no way.

Colossians 3:12–14:

> **Tenderhearted Mercy**—Barbara's husband was diagnosed with lung cancer. He had been a chain smoker. The doctors were not giving her much hope about him returning home after his surgery. She was prompted by God to lay her hand on him and pray with expectation. Three weeks later her husband had returned home with a changed prognosis that he had a miraculous turnaround. Barbara knew God had mercy on her husband. Now it was her turn to show mercy, for his mother came to stay with them for a week and was placing heavy demands on Barbara.
>
> **Humility**—Katie boasted about how wonderful her new job was. It happened to be the one Alice had applied for first but did not get. They were close friends, but Katie's selfishness

did not allow room for her to be sensitive to Alice's feelings. God had helped Alice to understand how Katie's boasting was a cover-up for her low self-esteem, so she did not reprimand Katie for being so inconsiderate when she knew it was Alice's dream job and goal for years. As a matter of fact, Alice provided some useful material for Katie to use in her new position.

1 Corinthians 13:1–8:

Love does not envy—*Kelly and Emily filled out adoption papers at the same time. It has been two years since Emily had her baby. Although Kelly cries at night sometimes, God brings comfort and reassurance to her that her day is coming. In the meantime, Kelly is surprised that God's love in her has enabled her to actually spend time with Emily and her baby without being envious. She is amazed by the inner strength God is providing.*

Does not rejoice in iniquity, but rejoices in the truth—*Anthony had raped Cathy and another girl in college. Both were young and too embarrassed to reveal what had happened to them. Somehow they blamed themselves for not being in the right place at the right time. Although some time had elapsed, the other girl revealed in a counseling session what Anthony had done to her. He was finally arrested. An appeal was posted for other women who may have been raped to step forward. God had brought such deliverance to Cathy she spoke up about what he had done to her, but it was not with bitter retaliation. She was not rejoicing over his being punished in jail either, for she had to forgive him a long time ago so she could go on with her life. However, she was rejoicing over how God had intervened to protect others and how He brought the truth out. She couldn't believe her own attitude!*

There is such freedom in yielding to God when relating to others. He has a way of doing exceedingly above what we can ask or even think. We do not even understand why we are behaving in certain ways. We are puzzled but pleased to see the evidence of God in us. On the contrary, it grieves His Spirit when we place more importance on others above Him. He loves them too. He loves all of His creation. Consequently, He knows you will have to operate out of your own fleshly reserve when you do not come to Him first to fill your love tank. Eventually you will be calling on Him to come and rescue you or the others involved.

I thought I knew this. I had experienced much torture when the Lord had me write a previous book. I was so concerned about not appearing prideful before others. I was so concerned about not being a poor testimony. I was so concerned about what other people had to say: "Oh, she's written a book now. Who does she think she is?" These thoughts had me paralyzed in obeying what I felt the Lord wanted me to do. It was not until I learned, to a greater degree, the love of God that I was set free from having to please everyone else. I had to stop putting them before Him. I had to stop putting myself before Him. It saddened my heart to know this is what I was doing. It is a battle, especially when you care so much about people and your loved ones. Remember, He is not promoting neglect of them but is blessing them by your being better equipped to love them in the way they need it.

There is such freedom in this agápe love, but are you walking around in bondage? "Oh, what does she think? What does he say? Oh, I must go join that class so I can be in the popular group. Oh, wait a minute, they switched over there. Let me get over there. I want to be in with the main crowd—I want to be loved." So you may run around and do things God never called you to do. So you are frustrated and tired, and you are getting mad at God because you are saying, "God, you're putting too much on me!" God is saying, "I never called you to do that. Again, you are running around putting all these relationships before Me. You are so concerned about getting your love tank filled in your own way. I never told you to do that." Jesus wants to fill your love tank with His sincere agápe love and have it overflow so much in your life that it is automatically going to flow back to Him and to others, even your enemies.

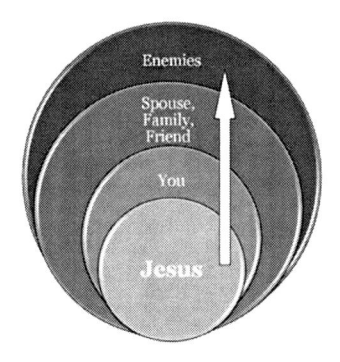

John 14:15 (KJV) says, *"If you love me, keep my commandments."* If you want to try to show God how much you love Him, just keep the two commandments we have been focusing on in regards to *receiving* and *giving* love. On these two commandments hang everything else. Just obey the first commandment before the second! There is godly wisdom as to why they are in that order. Romans 5:5 (NLT) says, *"And this hope will not lead to disappointment. For we know how dearly God loves us, because he has given us the Holy Spirit to fill our hearts with his love."*

You have God's Holy Spirit. Isaiah 11:2 lets us know God's Spirit is the Spirit of wisdom, understanding, counsel, might, knowledge, and reverential fear. What else do you need? What else do you need to handle relational situations every day? Do you need wisdom? Do you need understanding? Do you need counsel? What should you do? God's Spirit is able to give that to you. Do you need might? Do you need power—power beyond yourself to deal with abuse or things that are just not fair? Do you need the power to withstand or to uphold? Do you need power to overcome and have victory? As a Christian, you have this power! The world doesn't have this love or its power. Are you living your life in your own power? God is trying to show you how much He loves you. You can stifle His attempts to do so by your own self-preservation.

Self-Preservation

Eleanor had been placed in leadership at her church and was doing very well. She was excited for how she was able to contribute and help others. The ministry had become very fulfilling for her, so much so that she decided not to follow her husband, Ralph, to a different church. Ralph wanted to attend a different church because he was not pleased with the present one. Eleanor and Ralph's relationship had been declining for years. She felt she had better look out for herself, because who knew what may be in the future for both of them.

Roberta has heard rumors her department is going to be dissolved. Her husband has been unemployed for two years, and there has been much strain financially in their home. She cannot afford to lose her job too. Roberta begins to inform her boss of the mistakes Judith is making so if a decision has to be made between the two, he will naturally decide to keep Roberta for the new project being developed.

Doris was told by her mother, "You should always put money aside in a separate account in case your marriage does not last." Doris listened to her mother and has been able to put money aside by pretending the groceries totaled a certain amount. The total always included extra for her, just in case of a "rainy day."

Reflecting back on the two commandments (not suggestions), Matthew 22:39 stated, *"You shall love your neighbor as yourself."* Jesus, who created the human race (John 1:1–2), knew people normally love themselves and are self-centered. Since people love themselves, they are going to do what is best for them. Likewise, Jesus wanted them to look out for others in the same way they would look out for themselves.

There are people who have been wounded in such a way that it has caused them to not love themselves in a healthy way. It is easy to

Dropped but Not Broken

discover when people do not love themselves, for they also find it hard to love someone else. You have heard it said, "Hurting people hurt people." It is not biblical or healthy for you to not love yourself. One extreme is to be preoccupied with yourself all the time and have little concern for others. The other extreme is to despise yourself and be preoccupied all the time with what others think of you. Both are not what Jesus is saying in this passage.

Please understand there is a difference between when self is controlled by your old fleshly nature and when it is controlled by the Holy Spirit of God. You may feel this is straining at a gnat or is a play on words. However, it has become a stumbling block for many women who need to be set free. So time is being taken now to understand this Second Commandment for those who may need it.

Some Christians talk as if it is godly to hate yourself. There is teaching that leaves a person with the thought that you must desecrate self, deny self totally, and just blow self up! You can almost picture a person pulling out a strap and striking herself over and over again for any fleshly ways that may surface. It is as if this is the pathway to holiness. You begin to think you are more godly when you perceive yourself this way. Does it make sense to believe you can constantly hate yourself and then turn around and love someone else? Most of the time, when you hate yourself, you will find it easier to pull someone else apart. The very thing you hate about yourself will be the focus of criticism in someone else. It's like that old saying, "Misery likes company."

The lifestyle of holiness is accomplished by bringing self (also referred to as flesh) under the control of the Holy Spirit. It is He who produces holiness in you supernaturally. It is true you must deny self and submit to His control, but it is not true you must develop some type of hate for yourself because of your weaknesses. Paul did not like that his flesh got out of control at times, but he did not promote self-loathing (Rom. 7:14–25). Jesus wholeheartedly loves you. He wants you to have the right perspective about yourself so you can love others in the same manner that you love yourself.

You may be saying right now, "I do not love myself." This happens when you do not understand God's love for you and how precious you are to Him. Maybe you feel you are not experiencing his love on a daily basis as you perceive others are doing. Somehow you believe a lie that you are not special too. God is faithfully working on your behalf, but somehow you do not see how He is opening doors for you and making a way for you. Just because you do not feel His love, that does not mean His love is not there. If this mind-set continues, you will not be able to love others, and you will block others from loving you.

Unconsciously, if you do not believe you deserve to be loved or you are so flawed that no one will love you, you will get just what you believe. Your attitude and actions will sabotage any efforts another makes to show you love. This includes God Himself, who is constantly showering His love and grace upon you each day. If this is a blockage for you, stop and ask the Lord to deliver you from this mind-set. Ask Him to repair your heart so you can love from the inside out. Ask Him to help you love yourself in a healthy, balanced manner, not to extremes as mentioned previously. If you need to forgive yourself for something you did in the past, and it is hindering your love walk, then do so. Pray 1 John 1:9 from your heart and trust God to do just what He has said in this Scripture. If He is willing to forgive and forget your sin, you should as well.

Again, what you see in the passage from Jesus is, "You shall love your neighbor *as yourself.*" Jesus addressed love between the two of you in the First Commandment. Now, in the Second Commandment, He is addressing how you should love others in the same way you love yourself. He is not assuming that you hate yourself, but that you love yourself. Otherwise, He would be saying, "Now I want you to hate others in the same way you hate yourself." He would never say that! There needs to be a healthy balance in loving yourself.

In God's kingdom, when you are growing in your understanding of how much God loves you, you will begin by the power of the Holy Spirit to love who you are *in Him*—not apart from Him. You begin to stop tearing yourself down and stop trying to be all things to all people. You finally get it that God is pleased with you, and that is what matters. You stop trying to look like and be someone else, because God's love is transforming you into a beautiful person, and you see it! This is not making you prideful but more confident and secure in Christ. Should your confidence tip over into pride, the Holy Spirit will convict you of it, which provides even more security as you trust His leading. This has nothing to do with outward appearance. It is the beauty of God's indwelling Spirit. Remember in Galatians, chapter 5, the fruit of the Spirit is love. Also, 2 Corinthians 3:17 lets you know that where the Spirit of the Lord is, there is freedom. You are free to be who God has made you to be. You like yourself and God's plan for you. You learn to appreciate your personal relationship with Him, and He makes you feel good about yourself. So much more can be said about this. Hopefully you are getting the picture.

God did not send His Son into the world to condemn you (John 3:17). Jesus came that you may have life and have it more abundantly (John 10:10). It is as if Jesus is saying, "I love you very much. You are unique in how I made you. Now just be who I made you to be! Be yourself." When you get this understanding, you will be able to love others to a higher degree, because you will allow them to be free in Christ as well. You will extend His grace to them and love them in a way not humanly possible, because you want them to walk in the same supernatural love you are experiencing. You will learn to be yourself (all pretenses and masks removed) and you will want them to be free to be themselves too. If Christians would live in this way, a true revival would take place in this land. God's children would have love for God, for others, and for themselves.

However, when self is controlled by your old fleshly nature there is always some comparison or competition with another. You cannot walk in the freedom of being yourself, because you want to be or to have what you see another possess. When this fleshly self is dominating, you are not going to allow someone else to invade and snatch away what you feel you deserve. In the end, you are determined to take care of yourself. You are not truly concerned about doing what is best for the other person (as Jesus commanded). You see that in the body of Christ when one congregation boasts of being better than another congregation. This pastor is better than another pastor. With this attitude, there is no mutual support but competition and a fleshly looking out for one's self. If you were Satan, what would you target to try to destroy God's will on earth? Would it not be God's agápe love displayed on earth? Satan has gone rampant not only in the world but now in the church. A majority of Christians do not understand how to love one another with agápe love. The enemy is really kicking up a ruckus.

So there is a difference in what Jesus is saying about self and what the world (even some churches) are saying about self. One produces spiritual freedom and a joy of "Christ in me," while the other produces spiritual bondage and a fretting over "only me." You are not to hate yourself, but you are not to think more highly of yourself than you should either (Rom. 12:3).

Now let's get back to self-preservation. Self-preservation is a predominant concern for self. God's Word addresses this mind-set. Second Corinthians 5:15 (NKJV) says, *"And he died for all that those who live should no longer live for themselves but for him who died and rose again."* First Corinthians 10:24 (KJV) states, *"Let no man seek his own, but every man another's wealth."* James 3:16 (NLT) says, *"For wherever there is jealousy and selfish ambition, there you will find disorder and evil of every kind."* So you were not created to live for yourself.

Remember how 1 Corinthians 13:1–13 described God's agápe love? God's love is long-suffering and is kind. God's love is not jealous, not boastful, not arrogant, not rude, not selfish, not resentful, does not think evil, rejoices in truth, and bears all things. Did you hear that? Bears all things. I do not even want a paper cut. Believes all things, hopes all things, and endures all things. Do you remember how Galatians 5:22–23 stated that when God's love is operating in you there is love, joy, peace, patience, kindness, goodness, faithfulness, gentleness, and self-control? However, when self is in control you find sexual immorality, impurity, lustful pleasures, idolatry, sorcery, hostility, quarrelling, jealousy, outbursts of anger, selfish ambition, dissension, division, envy, drunkenness, wild parties, and other sins like these (Gal. 5:19–21). These also result when human love, apart from God's agápe love, is functioning. This is a big difference, isn't it?

Christians can quote major sins such as being involved in idolatry, adultery, sexual sin, jealousy, and hatred. At the same time, do you know that whenever you are operating out of self, it is just as bad? It is sin, because it is all centered on "me, myself, and I." This is the very thing that caused Satan to fall. God opened my eyes to something I want you to understand now. Become sensitive to the subtle trap of self-preservation. I have seen that most Christians are not even aware when they have this mind-set. Self-preservation is when you have a mind-set to safeguard or protect yourself. Someone may say, "What is wrong with that?" What is wrong is that this mind-set will hinder your trusting and being dependent upon God to safeguard and protect you. You will unknowingly try to handle things yourself, instead of trusting God to handle them. Additionally, when you constantly think about yourself and are constantly concerned about yourself, you are in the flesh. Being in the flesh will ultimately result in sin. Romans 7:18 (NKJV) says, *"For I know that in me (that is, in my flesh) nothing good dwells; for to will is present with me, but how to perform what is good I do not find."* So avoid self-preservation like a plague—it is a trap!

No good thing dwells in my flesh. I did not understand until God revealed it to me that when I was functioning in self-preservation, trying to preserve myself, I was operating in self. It was all about me. It was not about my Savior. As one who had always been a people pleaser, I decided one day to stop pleasing everyone else and start taking better care of me. I said to myself, "I am not going to let anyone step on me now. I am going to protect myself. I am not going to let others get over on me. They are taking advantage of my kindness and generosity." God showed me it was self-defense and self-preservation. It was all about me! When the Lord showed this to me, it broke my heart. It may not seem deliberate, but self-preservation is about you meeting your needs. Where is God?

God does not want us to be that weak and messed up. I was messed up. I'm serious. I was truly messed up. I know Christian women who easily enter into self-pity and self-flagellation. Flagellation is where you put yourself down all the time or are criticizing yourself constantly. Where is your focus when you do this? Self. Even self-righteousness is about self. Are you easily offended? Who are you thinking about when you are easily offended? Self. What about when you are bossy. Who are you thinking about when you get bossy? Yourself—because you want it your way.

Here are other ways you may operate in self. Are you self-conscious? Is self-complacency in you? Do you regularly get into self-pity? It is still self—just like these: self-seeking, self-indulgence, or self-defense.

Why are you impatient? Have you ever been impatient in a line in a grocery store? What are you thinking about? "Why does she have to get in front of me?" Who are you thinking about? Self. What about shyness?

Yes, even shyness. Why are you so shy? Again, you are thinking about yourself. You do not want people to think badly of you, or you do not want people to hurt you. Do you see how you can be so wrapped up in yourself? Why do you grumble? Again, things are not going your way. "Doesn't she know you don't do it that way?" Right? What about being irritable? I know I may be stepping on your toes, but you have to understand my toes are sore too. Oversensitive? I have been a very sensitive person, to the point I would get on my own nerves. Again, this would lead to concentrating on self.

The one thing I had to do when the Lord began to reveal this was to accept the truth and recognize when I was operating in self. When I started really acknowledging when I was operating in self versus operating in my Savior's love and under the control of His Spirit, I started to be set free.

Understanding God's love and acceptance of you is freeing! When I started to not be so preoccupied with other people's opinions and expectations, I began to like myself. If God's love for me was not based on performance, why should I allow others to put me in prison by their demands? It is freeing.

Another thing—being resentful. Why do you get resentful, and why do you fret? Can it be because you are concerned something isn't going to turn out your way? Do you see how much self can dominate your life? Many relational problems stem from selfish desires and demands.

James 4:1–10 lets us know what is causing the quarrels and fights in relationships. Why do you have problems in your love relationships? They come from the evil desires that war within you. We have certain desires and wants and expectations—self. It says you want what you do not have. So what do you do? You scheme and kill to get it. You have something that you desire, and you want it so badly that you're willing to scheme, manipulate, and do what you have to do to get it, even to the point of killing for it. Now you may say, "I would never murder anyone." Well, what about your mouth? Have you ever murdered anybody with that weapon? You are jealous of what others have, and you cannot get it, so you fight and wage war to take it away from them. Look at the Scripture further. You do not have what you want because you don't ask God for it. You do not turn to God to meet your needs. You may look to other people. You may look to fulfill your own needs, but you do not have what you need because you have not turned to Jesus.

You may be saying, "No, Paula, I do turn to God." What does the passage say? Even when you ask, you do not get, because your motives are all wrong. So maybe you pray, but your motives are wrong. Your focus is still on you. So what are you to learn? Why are you having so many problems in your love relationships? It is because you have some expectations and desires and pleasures, and you want them met. You expect your spouse, family, and friends to do what you want them to do. In all honesty, isn't this true? When they do not meet your needs as expected, your love for them is not expressed so easily. Also, you may go into a mode of self-preservation concerning them. You may unconsciously feel they do not deserve to be lavished with your love. You may not say it, but your attitude and actions may show it.

The passage stated that you do not receive because your motives are all wrong—you want only what will give you pleasure. God is basically, for many Christians, a bellhop. "Now, God, go do this and fix her and have him do this." When we look at God in this way, we get upset or confused with Him because He does not do everything we want Him to do. We want Him to meet our pleasures and our desires.

What do you think the scriptures mean when they say the Spirit of God placed within us is filled with envy? What is God saying? God is saying, "I love you so much. I deeply desire that the Spirit of love I have placed in you will return to Me. I have placed in you My love. Return that love to Me. Each time you say no, you are committing adultery with the Lord. You are giving that love to other people and to other things, trying to complete your own self. God is saying, "Come back to Me. The jealousy I have for you is not like a human jealousy. I want to love you. I want to commune with you. I want you to know Me. I want you to walk in My power. Why are you going over there? I'll meet your needs. You commit adultery by leaving Me for others. You have left your first love. Come back to Me!"

James, in chapter 4, continues to let you know He gives even more grace to stand against such evil desires. God opposes the proud but favors the humble. So, humble yourself before God. God is saying, "Do you know what? I understand you. I know the mistakes you have made in your human relationships. You keep putting your human and natural relationships before Me, and you commit adultery all the time. You will not spend time with Me; you do not come talk with Me. You do not fellowship with Me. You do not give Me a chance to even show you My power, because you are trying to meet your needs. You are working it out on your own. You are manipulating things. You are killing and striking. You are working a lot. You have not even come to Me. But if you will, I will have pardon and show My grace to you." God's grace is His abundant blessings and empowerment. He will lavish it upon you if you are humble. If you are proud and keep on trying to meet your needs yourself (self-preservation), you will never understand agápe love or operate in it.

This same chapter tells you how to humble yourself. Resist the devil. When the devil tells you to try to get your own needs met, by you doing something or by looking to another person, resist him. When you resist him, he will flee from you. What else do you have to do to humble yourself? Come close to God, and God will come close to you. "You know what, Lord? I realize right now what I'm trying to do is really about self. My self-preservation is involved here. It's not really about You. It's not really about Your will. I have my own agenda. I recognize now, Lord, that it is even my agenda when I try self-abasement. Even when I try to preserve myself so people will not think wrong or talk about me, I am still wrapped up in self."

So you have to acknowledge when self is the focus and come before God and say, "Lord, forgive me. My thinking has been wrong. I am still concerned about me. All I need to do is think about what You are telling me to do, believe it, step out, and trust You. You will give me the power to do what You want me to do. I do not need to be concerned whether Sally, Sue, Mary, or whoever has an opinion about it. If I am obedient to You, I will see Your agápe love working in the whole situation." What you have to do is draw nigh to God and say something to the effect of, "God help me. I slipped into self-preservation again. Help me, Lord. I need You right now." And if you do that, He says He will do what? He will draw nigh to you. He knows everything about you. That person cannot do for you what He is able to do for you. Brad Pitt, Denzel Washington, it does not matter. They do not have it over Him.

Dropped but Not Broken

God is telling you to stop indulging in that which is causing you to walk in self. Whatever you are doing, stop and humble yourself before Him. Acknowledge too if your self-preservation is putting demands on others. Are you putting so much pressure on your husband that when he gets overtime, he likes it because it is a lot easier to work there than it is to come home and work for you? Are you placing unrealistic expectations on your children? Be sensitive to when self is rearing its ugly head. You can become prideful in what you expect your children to accomplish. It can be a concern about yourself and how you look and how you are perceived. This can be with teachers, in church, or in the community. It can all be self-preservation.

Now, let me tell you. When you start to love from the inside out, you are going to get a little confused, because you may be so used to your flesh dominating. I am going to tell you up front, you may even get frustrated or discouraged as you start practicing this. It is not natural for us to walk in God's agápe love. It is natural for us to walk according to our selfish desires. If you would just do what He tells you to do in James and recognize when your flesh is trying to take control, you will live a much better life.

You can tell when your flesh is dominating, because you will lose your inner peace. Whenever you lose your peace with God, that is a warning signal to watch out and see if your flesh desires fulfillment. The Holy Spirit is going to let you know, and what you have to do is honestly acknowledge it before God. When you acknowledge it and humble yourself before God, He will deliver you. He will provide His agápe love so you will not be out for self but for others. You may find yourself saying, "Whoa, I wouldn't even give her the time of day, and now I have such compassion for her."

Be sensitive to when you are operating in the flesh and when you are operating in the Spirit. You can go into Galatians, chapter 5, and you can go into 1 Corinthians 13, and you can start using them as a measurement to see, "Why am I making this decision? Why do I want this? Why am I irritated because this didn't happen?" Start asking the Lord to give you wisdom and understanding as to why you have lost your peace. If you have lost your peace, you need to try to find out whether you are operating in your flesh. Is there something you desire or some pleasure you thought you were going to have, and all of a sudden it is not being fulfilled? Soon you will recognize more often when your flesh raises its ugly head.

If you are going to walk in agápe love, you will have to walk in humility and not in self. I just want you to be aware of this fact. You will be humbled over and over again. At times you may feel it is so unjust for you to have to be the one to reconcile a relationship. You may ask, "Why do I have to humble myself? Why do I have to go when I am the victim?" You may be the victim of unfair circumstances. Yet, God is calling you to rely on Him and not to handle it yourself. The same resurrection power that raised Jesus from the dead will be operating in and through you (1 Cor. 6:14). So, yes, you will have to humble yourself. If you have done something, you may have to go to someone and say, "You know what? I'm sorry. I really thought this would work my way, and now I see your way is better."

As one who has begun to really live like this, I must say there is no other way to continuously walk in freedom concerning your relationships. I am not saying it is easy. It is hard at times. It is hard because your flesh is going to be screaming! You can do so through the power of the Spirit and God's love. Turn to Jesus and let him give you the power to humble yourself time after time. I am telling you, once you practice humility, you will begin to see the godly results it brings. You will be able to see God do new things in your relationships. I'm telling you the truth. To the world this is crazy, but in the kingdom it is the way to have victory in your relationships. The Bible reveals Jesus's humility for mankind, and you will display humility as well when this lifestyle becomes yours. The funny thing is, you will not end up being perceived as a wimp but as a mighty woman of God.

Will everyone respond the way you desire? No. But that is all right because God will give you the power to make it through. Even when your spouse, family, and friends are not acting correctly, God will give you strength. You will be able to say, "Whew. I can make it. It's all right." Then when you have done all, just stand.

Having Done All, Just Stand

Rose could not believe Violet was avoiding her again. Rose did everything she could do to resolve the conflict they had last year. Violet was stubbornly refusing to extend forgiveness to Rose. Rose was frustrated by Violet's behavior but realized there was nothing more she could do.

Beth always thought of herself as a loving person, but God knew her thoughts, and sometimes they did not always express love. She was called by God to trust Jesus as her Savior and Lord at the age of ten at a Jack Wyrtzen rally. She claimed her life verse to be Ephesians 4:32, which states, *"Be kind to one another, tenderhearted, forgiving one another, even as God for Christ's sake hath forgiven you."* She found it easy to be kind and tenderhearted, but forgiving had been a lifetime struggle for her. As she advanced in age, she would still find herself in His refining fire being molded and made to be obedient to His Word. God began to show her more deeply how much He loved her and how His son died an awful death on a cross for her sins long before she was born. She knew she should be following His example by forgiving others, knowing we love because He first loved us. What an awesome loving God, she thought. She felt God nudging her to forgive those who did not agree with her or who did not live up to the biblical standards she thought they should. Beth learned she must forgive someone in her heart, and not just in her head or by words.

After many years of estrangement, God moved her brother to make amends with her and his family. Even though she was showing him acts of kindness and what she thought was true love during a division in the family, it took God moving in both of them to bring them together in His love. God knew Beth's heart was not right, even though it appeared she was a loving sister. She was finally blessed to extend forgiveness as God through Christ had done for her. She still has some others to forgive but is allowing God to lead her in the way He would have her to do this.

Beth's brother recently went home to be with the Lord. She was so thankful to God that in the last several months of his life on earth, they were able to share familial and Christian love. His favorite hymn was "It Is Well with My Soul." She had the privilege to sing to him just before he died. Beth is so grateful to God, for His never-ending love allowed her to have peace and comfort at her brother's home going. She experienced joy and sorrow meeting together, and it was sweet. She reflected upon how God is good all the time, and His timing is always perfect.

Ephesians 6:13 (NKJV) states, *"Therefore take up the whole armor of God, that you may be able to withstand in the evil day, and having done all, to stand."* There are times in relationships where conflicts occur, and things get out of control. You must know how to respond to conflict, and having done all you can do, just stand (trusting God). What relationship does not have conflict? Conflict is normal and necessary for healthy relationships. Now some may say they never have conflict, and they do not agree with this statement. It would be something to dig deeper to see if the two involved are truly transparent and open in each area of the relationship. Each person is designed differently by God, with unique characteristics and personalities. It is learning to accept and deal with the other's differences whereby we grow. You may have heard the saying, "If both are alike, then one is unnecessary." It's not realistic to think two people can agree on everything at all times. Therefore, learning to deal with conflict and to not avoid it is important.

Relationships suffer when conflict is not handled correctly. However, when conflict is handled correctly, both parties have an opportunity for growth. Since no two people are alike, it's good to have some insight in this area. There are many things that can cause a conflict: convictions, ideas, desires, expectations, goals, etc. When conflicts arise, there is a root issue brewing underneath. It is normally some need for respect, security, or intimacy. It can be a need to feel valued or supported or understood or safe. This is important, for a person may nitpick over some surface issue that is not the issue at all. An example of this is a person arguing over a cup left on the table when the real issue is one of not feeling validated. Conflicts are more than a difference of opinion. A conflict occurs when there is a true or perceived threat. Since a threat is perceived, strong emotions will usually accompany conflicts. A person's view and beliefs will play a major part in how the conflict is resolved.

The worst thing to do is to avoid conflict at all costs. If some earlier relational conflict has left you traumatized, it is more likely you will be fearful to get involved in any conflict. Know that all conflicts do not have to end badly. You must pray and ask the Lord to help you overcome feelings of anxiety, fear, danger, and humiliation when a conflict occurs in your life. You do not want a conflict to fester over a long period of time.

Another thing you do not want to do is take up someone else's offense. It is easy to do when you are emotionally attached to someone. Their pain becomes your pain too. If their affliction causes them to become weak, it is natural to want to step in and fight for them. There is a time for righteous indignation, but you must seek God as to when it is appropriate for you to step in for another. You may get in God's way. He is always growing both parties, and you may hinder a work He is doing. Be careful. *"He who passes by and meddles in a quarrel not his own is like one who takes a dog by the ears"* (Prov. 26:17, NKJV).

If you are in need of forgiveness for some act you have committed, seek forgiveness right away. Do not delay unless the time and place are not appropriate. Do not make excuses for your behavior. See and call it as God would. Be honest and forthright in your dealings. Do not say, "I am sorry *if...*" Do not accuse the other person when you are confessing to them and asking for their forgiveness. "I would have... had you not..." "You're the reason I..." You will only make matters worse. State specifically what you are in need of forgiveness for—do not water down or minimize your behavior. Acknowledge the hurt or pain afflicted upon the other person. Validate their feelings. Speak to each person who was offended if several people are involved. If necessary, make restitution for your actions. Do what is necessary to bring healing to the relationship, whether it feels good to you or not. *"He that covereth his sins shall not prosper: But whoso confesseth and forsaketh them shall have mercy"* (Prov. 28:13, KJV).

If someone has offended or hurt you, and it is something you just cannot overlook and put behind you, then you need to go to them and let them know they have offended you. They may honestly not be aware that something they said or did hurt you. *"Dear brothers and sisters, if another believer is overcome by some sin, you who are godly should gently and humbly help that person back onto the right path. And be careful not to fall into the same temptation yourself. Share each other's burdens, and in this way obey the law of Christ. If you think you are too important to help someone, you are only fooling yourself. You are not that important"* (Gal. 6:1–3, NLT). This is not an easy thing to do and must be done prayerfully and humbly. Here are some things to avoid when dealing with conflict:

1. Do not let your emotions and anger become explosive toward the other person. *"What is causing the quarrels and fights among you? Don't they come from the evil desires at war within you"* (James 4:1, NLT)? Ask the Lord to help you "respond" and not "react." (Be nondefensive, calm, and respectful.) When your emotions and behavior are under control, you can communicate your needs in a way that does not threaten others. Communicate your needs clearly. Do not lash out or go for the other's throat (James 1:20).
2. Do not become resentful and withdraw yourself, leaving with feelings of rejection. Do not shut down; this is not beneficial.
3. Do not use the offense as a weapon against the other person. Do not allow it to be a weapon used against you—such as thoughts of your being unacceptable or unworthy. Guard your thoughts (2 Cor. 10:5).
4. Do not be unwilling to try to understand the other person's point of view.
5. Do not lie or cover up your true feelings. Deal with the conflict truthfully.
6. Be careful of unrighteous nonverbal communication (i.e., facial expressions and body movements).
7. Do not run around telling others who were not involved, trying to get them to see your point of view. You should first discuss this just between you and the person who offended you.

Dropped but Not Broken

Here are some things to pray over and practice when any conflict arises:

1. Seek God's wisdom on the cause of the hurt. Ask Him to reveal if you have been overly sensitive, critical, or negative, or if you had unrealistic expectations. We all have blind spots. Was there something you should or should not have done? It would be good if each person would acknowledge their part in the erosion of the relationship. *"Every way of a man is right in his own eyes: But the Lord pondereth the hearts"* (Prov. 21:2, KJV). *"Do not judge others, and you will not be judged. For you will be treated as you treat others. The standard you use in judging is the standard by which you will be judged. "And why worry about a speck in your friend's eye when you have a log in your own? How can you think of saying to your friend, 'Let me help you get rid of that speck in your eye,' when you can't see past the log in your own eye? Hypocrite! First get rid of the log in your own eye; then you will see well enough to deal with the speck in your friend's eye"* (Matt. 7:1–5, NLT).
2. Eliminate pain, agony, and distress by dealing with things quickly while you are with the individual who offended you (Matt. 5:25).
3. Choose the right time and place to have your conversation. Try to avoid confronting someone in front of others who are not involved. Treat them the same way you would want to be treated. *"If another believer sins against you, go privately and point out the offense. If the other person listens and confesses it, you have won that person back. But if you are unsuccessful, take one or two others with you and go back again, so that everything you say may be confirmed by two or three witnesses. If the person still refuses to listen, take your case to the church. Then if he or she won't accept the church's decision, treat that person as a pagan or a corrupt tax collector"* (Matt. 18:15–17, NLT).
4. Listen to what the other person is saying instead of just being ready to fire back what you are thinking or feeling. Do not interrupt. Assumptions can lead to deeper conflicts. It is important to have a discussion and not presume anything or feel you "already know" what another is thinking or feeling. Ask questions if needed. You want to make sure

you truly understand what they are saying. *"He who answers before listening—that is folly and his shame"* (Prov. 18:13, NIV). You must allow your offender to be totally honest and transparent with you without your attacking his/her character. You must listen and learn.
5. If you have to approach the other person, try to use "I" first instead of "you." Using the word "you" first is like pointing a finger at them and will make them defensive. For example: "I may not have understood correctly, did you mean to say…" "I am feeling hurt by what was said…" "I originally thought that …"
6. Separate the person from the problem, and do not attack him or her personally. You want to deal with the problem that caused the conflict. Stick to the problem.
7. Let your motivation be to resolve the conflict not to win or be right. If winning is your only focus, you have already lost. Fight for a resolution. Try to get to the point of "Oh, I see what you are saying." "I thought you meant… I thought you were saying … I thought you had… I thought you were blaming me for…" Let go of preconceived notions and be open.
8. Watch the words you use. It is amazing how a certain word may trigger a strong reaction, and just by changing a word, the conflict can be ended. For example: "a lie" is strong; the term "discrepancy" may be used until you know for sure a deliberate effort was made to deceive. Just a change in words may throw water on the fire. *"Do not let any unwholesome talk come out of your mouths, but only what is helpful for building others up according to their needs, that it may benefit those who listen"* (Eph. 4:29, NIV).
9. Focus on the situation at hand; do not bring in past offenses and hurts. Try to offer a solution for what is taking place now. Do not pile up old mistakes. *"I, even I, am he who blots out your transgressions, for my own sake, and remembers your sins no more"* (Isa. 43:25, NIV).
10. Take the other person's needs into consideration. Try to see the conflict from their point of view. Look beyond the surface to their root issue (even if they do not understand what it is).

11. A soft answer (Prov. 15:1) and even humor at times will disarm your opponent.
12. If appropriate, seek a compromise without punishment or resentment. Don't make him/her pay for your not getting your way.
13. Be willing to forgive and not hold onto a grudge. Be open to finding solutions you may not have considered before. Be flexible. *"Take heed to yourselves: If thy brother trespass against thee, rebuke him; and if he repent, forgive him"* (Luke 17:3, KJV).
14. If it will not betray a confidence, have others pray for the conflict to be resolved as well.

If both individuals come to a solution over the conflict, then reaffirm one another. If appropriate, reaffirm your affection and love—at least brotherly love with a brother or sister in Christ. This can be done with a handshake or hug. Both should have reached some type of understanding. Before going your separate ways, *each one* should try to:

1. Respectfully repeat what the other has said to make sure you heard correctly and do indeed understand. "What I am hearing is …" "Sounds like you are saying …"
2. Summarize what is being asked of you. "It is my understanding then that you would like for me to …"

Hopefully, each will be sincere in respecting one another's opinions, and there will be no judgment made toward the other or any root of bitterness springing up later (Heb. 12:15). By no means should there be any retelling of what happened in private to others (unless agreed upon by both parties for a testimony to glorify God).

If a mediator is needed to resolve the conflict, try to get someone who is agreeable to both parties. This person must be neutral and must be one who will not show favoritism. It is good to have a person who is biblically based so their advice is godly and not just opinion. Hopefully, the mediator will be able to listen and then provide wise solutions and options for both involved. This person may be used to help open the eyes of one who has stubbornly stuck his or her heels in and will not move.

If you cannot come to a resolution, agree to disagree. It takes two for a conflict, so do not engage any further. Having done all you can do (and make sure that you have), let it go, and keep it before God in prayer. Allow Him to give you wisdom and to work on the other person involved. Trust Him for a good outcome. Maybe the conflict can be resolved by the solution taking place in several steps rather than one big leap. This is especially helpful where trust has been broken. When step one has been completed successfully, then you can proceed to step two and so on. Having the solution in bite-size pieces may be more palatable for one involved. Do not anticipate doom; you may get just what you believe for. Instead, cast all of your cares upon the Lord and wait on Him (Ps. 55:22) for a good outcome. *"If it is possible, as much as depends on you, live peaceably with all men"* (Rom. 12:18, NKJV).

Although Christians have been forgiven of *all* their sins, they may fail to extend that forgiveness to others. You may find someone saying, "I forgive her, I just do not want to have anything to do with her again." Could you imagine God saying that about those He has forgiven? Of course He never would. He is forever wooing us to Himself. There are times when forgiveness is extended, and continued fellowship is not possible (cases of abuse, death of offender, etc.). There are times when even Christians will harden their hearts and refuse to forgive and be reconciled. You are not responsible for their actions but for your own obedience to the Lord.

Everything we do should be done for the glory of God. Our actions and decisions should cause us to believe our Lord is rejoicing over us. Our goal in any conflict is restoration, not condemnation. There should be no twinge of revenge in your heart. You should be able to walk away with peace in your heart, regardless of the outcome, knowing you were obedient to the Lord. *"Live such good lives among the pagans that, though they accuse you of doing wrong, they may see your good deeds and glorify God on the day he visits us"* (1 Pet. 2:12, NIV). If the conflict was not resolved initially, always be prepared to receive the offender should he or she return like the prodigal's son in Scripture (Luke 15:11–32). When you have done everything you can do, just stand in faith.

Dropped but Not Broken

Here are some passages to encourage your faith. Look intently to see what you are instructed to do. Of course, be mindful of what you are not to do as well.

"Do not fret because of evil men or be envious of those who do wrong; for like the grass they will soon wither, like green plants they will soon die away. Trust in the Lord and do good; dwell in the land and enjoy safe pasture. Delight yourself in the Lord and he will give you the desires of your heart. Commit your way to the Lord; trust in him and he will do this: He will make your righteousness shine like the dawn, the justice of your cause like the noonday sun. Be still before the Lord and wait patiently for him; do not fret when men succeed in their ways, when they carry out their wicked schemes. Refrain from anger and turn from wrath; do not fret—it leads only to evil. For evil men will be cut off, but those who hope in the Lord will inherit the land" (Ps. 37:1–9, NIV).

"Do not repay anyone evil for evil. Be careful to do what is right in the eyes of everybody. If it is possible, as far as it depends on you, live at peace with everyone. Do not take revenge, my friends, but leave room for God's wrath, for it is written: 'It is mine to avenge; I will repay,' says the Lord. On the contrary: 'If your enemy is hungry, feed him; if he is thirsty, give him something to drink. In doing this, you will heap burning coals on his head.' Do not be overcome by evil, but overcome evil with good" (Rom. 12:17–21, NIV).

"Then Peter came to him and asked, 'Lord, how often should I forgive someone who sins against me? Seven times?' 'No, not seven times,' Jesus replied, 'but seventy times seven!' Therefore, the Kingdom of Heaven can be compared to a king who decided to bring his accounts up to date with servants who had borrowed money from him. In the process, one of his debtors was brought in who owed him millions of dollars. He couldn't pay, so his master ordered that he be sold—along with his wife, his children, and everything he owned—to pay the debt. But the man fell down before his master and begged him, 'Please, be patient with me, and I will pay it all.' Then his master was filled with pity for him, and he released him and forgave his debt. But when the man left the king, he went to a fellow servant who owed him a few thousand dollars. He grabbed him by the throat and demanded instant payment. His fellow servant fell down before him and begged for a little more time. 'Be patient with me, and I will pay it,' he pleaded. But his creditor wouldn't wait. He had the man arrested and put in prison until the debt could be paid in full. When some of the other servants saw this, they were very upset. They

went to the king and told him everything that had happened. Then the king called in the man he had forgiven and said, 'You evil servant! I forgave you that tremendous debt because you pleaded with me. Shouldn't you have mercy on your fellow servant, just as I had mercy on you?' Then the angry king sent the man to prison to be tortured until he had paid his entire debt. That's what my heavenly Father will do to you if you refuse to forgive your brothers and sisters from your heart" (Matt. 18:21–35, NLT).

"Don't have anything to do with foolish and stupid arguments, because you know they produce quarrels. And the Lord's servant must not quarrel; instead, he must be kind to everyone, able to teach, not resentful. Those who oppose him he must gently instruct, in the hope that God will grant them repentance leading them to a knowledge of the truth, and that they will come to their senses and escape from the trap of the devil, who has taken them captive to do his will" (2 Tim. 2:23–26, NIV).

Conflicts are indeed complicated, and the material here is just enough to keep them from getting worse. More severe conflicts may need a mediator(s) to help bring a resolution. One thing is for sure, the Lord requires you to forgive over and over again. He also requires you to forgive "as" He does. He warned in the Matthew passage above, that to neglect to do so will turn you over to be tortured. I have seen many a Christian who is tortured by unforgiveness and bitterness. They are inflicting more pain on themselves than on the offender. This is not what Christ died for. Even when you are working to restore a relationship, another question may rise, "Am I called to love when I don't even trust?"

Love When I Don't Even Trust?

Linda could not believe the request that had just fallen on her ears. Her mother wanted her to take in her younger sister until she could get back on her feet. Linda's younger sister was strung out on drugs and had just been released from jail. Linda was constantly bailing her out of trouble to alleviate stress on her mom. Linda loved her sister, but should she trust her in her own house and with a house key?

> *"Listen to my prayer, O God. Do not ignore my cry for help! Please listen and answer me, for I am overwhelmed by my troubles. My enemies shout at me, making loud and wicked threats. They bring trouble on me and angrily hunt me down. My heart pounds in my chest. The terror of death assaults me. Fear and trembling overwhelm me, and I can't stop shaking. Oh, that I had wings like a dove; then I would fly away and rest. It is not an enemy who taunts me—I could bear that. It is not my foes who so arrogantly insult me—I could have hidden from them. Instead, it is you—my equal, my companion, and close friend. What good fellowship we once enjoyed as we walked together to the house of God. But I will call on God, and the Lord will rescue me. Morning, noon, and night I cry out in my distress, and the Lord hears my voice. He ransoms me and keeps me safe from the battle waged against me, though many still oppose me. God, who has ruled forever, will hear me and humble them. Give your burdens to the Lord, and he will take care of you. He will not permit the godly to slip and fall. I am trusting you to save me"* (Ps. 55:1–23, NLT).

When you have been betrayed or traumatized in a relationship, you may find it hard to trust again. This is natural. The thing you want to avoid is getting stuck in self-preservation, which is also natural. Jesus did not die for you to be entangled again in a yoke of bondage (Gal. 5:1). Remember, you were created to be in relationship with God and others. You are made to *receive* and *give* love. This is supernatural. You live in a fallen world where things do not always go as you desire, for things on earth are not perfect and without sin as they are in Heaven.

Brokenness and forgiveness are vital parts of love. If you enter into any love relationship, you will find this to be true. A number of people will enter into your life to test and prove that your love is genuine. It is inevitable that someone is going to hurt you. If you are not careful, anger, resentment, fear, bitterness, and lack of trust will destroy you. They can cause you to live alone the rest of your life if you do not learn to forgive and trust again. The entire Christian faith is based on forgiveness. Did God have to forgive us? Was He forced to forgive? No, He did it freely and fully. You are a Christian because of God's forgiveness. *"Think of all the hostility he endured from sinful people; then you won't become weary and give up. After all, you have not yet given your lives in your struggle against sin"* (Heb. 12:3–4, NLT). *"If someone says, 'I love God,' and hates his brother, he is a liar; for he who does not love his brother whom he has seen, how can he love God whom he has not seen? And this commandment we have from Him: that he who loves God must love his brother also"* (1 John 4:20–21, NKJV).

Although all damaged relationships are not restored, will you allow yourself to forgive? Will you release that person and yourself from the prison of unforgiveness? It will take the love of God within you to set yourself free and to also free the other person. When you forgive, then your heart will have the capacity to trust again. He did not love the world because everyone in it was lovable, and you may be called on to love the unlovable as well. C. S. Lewis once said, "A proud man is always looking down on things and people; and, of course, as long as you're looking down, you can't see something that's above you."[3] As long as you are looking down on someone, you cannot look up (to God). You cannot do both at same time. *"Make allowance for each other's faults, and forgive anyone who offends you. Remember, the Lord forgave you, so you must forgive others. Above all, clothe yourselves with love, which binds us all together in perfect harmony"* (Col. 3:13–14, NLT).

This is a very complex subject and must be covered in prayer and in seeking wisdom from God. Here are some things to prayerfully ponder in trying to regain your trust level so future relationships will not be damaged by past hurts:

Dropped but Not Broken

- Understand there are risks and vulnerability in all human relationships.
- Realize trust can be broken instantly and may take some time to rebuild. Be patient with yourself. Accept that part of living is growing strong through hurts and pain.
- If you build up walls around yourself to keep others out, you will be in prison. Do not shelter yourself away from others; you need to stay connected no matter how much you may want to retreat in a closet.
- Refuse to be a victim. When given an invitation to a pity party, refuse.
- If you have been abused or raped, go to a biblical counselor (one who gives advice from the Word of God.) You have been severely traumatized and will need professional or pastoral help. Call Focus on the Family at 1-800-A-Family if you have no other resource for a counselor.
- For healing to start and trust to begin, you must open up and talk. You must face the situation and not keep it hidden. It will only grow in the dark like mold. Even writing your emotions out on a piece of paper will allow a release to take place.
- Appreciate who you are and learn to be authentic and transparent in your relationships. This may be fearful at first, but keep trying until you can do so without thinking about it.
- If a decision has been made to repair the relationship, let the offender know what you need to regain trust within the relationship. Everyone has different needs; do not assume they should know yours.
- Don't get caught up in believing other people know what is best for you. It's true they know what is best for them, but no one ultimately knows what's best for you but God. You don't want to set up others to fail again and drive the knife of distrust deeper.
- You were surprised by this, but God was not. What are you to learn from this? How can God get the glory out of this? There will be times in relationships when you will have every right to walk away having no guilt or shame, but when you stay and work on that relationship, you will

become a better person. You will have brought glory to God in a way you would never have if you had walked out. Your trust muscles will have a good workout as well (smile).
- God is just and will make all things right sooner or later. He knows what it is to be mistreated. *"He will not crush the weakest reed or put out a flickering candle. He will bring justice to all who have been wronged"* (Isa. 42:3, NLT). Trust Him even when it's hard to trust people.
- Save yourself the heartache of trying to make someone be what you want them to be.
- Don't make others pay for another person's mistake.
- Deal with your insecurities that may be causing you to be suspicious without cause. Take note if you are becoming paranoid and fearful of everyone.
- Don't try to force yourself to trust again by leaping right into another relationship with the opposite sex. Allow time to grieve and heal from the last relationship.
- If you decide to remain in a shell, what you have decided is to let the person who hurt you continue to hurt you. Say no to this.

Dr. Phil said something interesting, "Trust is not about how much you trust one person or another to do right or wrong. How much you trust another person is a function of how much you trust yourself to be strong enough to deal with their imperfections."[4] So overall it's not about trusting others; it is about trusting yourself to handle what others might do. You cannot control other people, but you can control yourself (through the power of the Holy Spirit). For trust to resurface, believe you will make a good decision the next time. Let God direct your steps and comfort you when needed in any relationship. Believe He is faithful and can change this around for your good. Cry out to Jesus, and you will learn to trust again. *"O God, listen to my cry! Hear my prayer! From the ends of the earth, I cry to you for help when my heart is overwhelmed. Lead me to the towering rock of safety, for you are my safe refuge, a fortress where my enemies cannot reach me. Let me live forever in your sanctuary, safe beneath the shelter of your wings"* (Ps. 61:1–4, NLT)!

"You have heard that it was said, 'You shall love your neighbor and hate your enemy.' But I say to you, love your enemies, bless those who curse you,

do good to those who hate you, and pray for those who spitefully use you and persecute you, that you may be sons of your Father in heaven; for He makes His sun rise on the evil and on the good, and sends rain on the just and on the unjust. For if you love those who love you, what reward have you? Do not even the tax collectors do the same? And if you greet your brethren only, what do you do more than others? Do not even the tax collectors do so? Therefore you shall be perfect, just as your Father in heaven is perfect" (Matt. 5:43–48, NKJV).

My heart is with you. I know what it is to be betrayed in trusted relationships. I have also matured and learned a lot from them. They became lessons I now praise and thank God for. Jesus knows what it is to be betrayed and left by his friends too. He also learned from the things He suffered. *"Even though Jesus was God's Son, he learned obedience from the things he suffered"* (Heb. 5:8, NLT). Let Him heal your broken heart and fill it with His agápe love. Believe what God has said over what Satan may be whispering to you. Belief in what God says produces faith. Belief in what Satan says produces fear. Christ died that you may have the victory over fear.

As we conclude this part of "Love Lens," I pray the light of God has passed through your mind and heart and has formed a clear image of what His love is in your relationships. You understand now how important it is to not just love in word or tongue but in deed and truth. It was discussed how the ones you love can easily become idols when you give undivided attention to them at the neglect of spending quality time with Jesus. In focusing on what love looks like, you have seen how self-preservation must be avoided if your relationships are going to grow. It was also important to cover some steps to take when conflicts arise. There will be times when you have done all you can do, and you must just wait on the Lord to move on the individual(s) involved. There may be times when you are called to love and forgive even when you don't trust. It does not mean you put yourself in harm's way, but you stay healthy spiritually and physically by not allowing bitterness to eat away at you. Overall, in looking at the horizontal relationships, Jesus's love and forgiveness is repeatedly covering you day after day, and you will have the opportunity day after day to extend the same to others. May you make the choice to sincerely love.

Advance on your journey to the next part of this book, "Love Light," that you may glow with this boundless love. *"Is not this the kind of fasting I have chosen: to loose the chains of injustice and untie the cords of the yoke, to set the oppressed free and break every yoke? Is it not to share your food with the hungry and to provide the poor wanderer with shelter—when you see the naked, to clothe him, and not to turn away from your own flesh and blood? Then your light will break forth like the dawn, and your healing will appear; then your righteousness will go before you, and the glory of the Lord will be your rear guard. Then you will call, and the Lord will answer; you will cry for help, and he will say: Here am I. "If you do away with the yoke of oppression, with the pointing finger and malicious talk, and if you spend yourselves in behalf of the hungry and satisfy the needs of the oppressed, then your light will rise in the darkness, and your night will become like the noonday"* (Isa. 58:6–10, NIV).

Smile; Jesus loves you!

Part 4

Love Light
"Daily Living It Out"

Part 4:
Love Light – "Daily Living It Out"

"You are the light of the world. A city that is set on a hill cannot be hidden. Nor do they light a lamp and put it under a basket, but on a lampstand, and it gives light to all who are in the house. Let your light so shine before men, that they may see your good works and glorify your Father in heaven."

(Matt. 5:14–16, NKJV)

Deflection from Devotion

Carmen felt she had been hit with a two-by-four as the Bible teacher's explanation pierced her heart. All along she felt God did not love her to the degree He had loved others. She always had to struggle and have nothing work out for her as others always seemed to be blessed. She just could not understand why even God seemed prejudiced. It never occurred to her, until the lesson today, that her doubt of God's love was propagated by her lack of spending time with Him. He was a stranger. She really did not know Him any more than a person she may pass on the street. So how could she know of His love? She wouldn't recognize it if He plastered it on a humongous billboard or announced it through an oversized bullhorn! She had so much desire for the "gifts" but not "The Giver" of the gifts. She was convinced she needed to spend time to know Him, and then she would have a heart open to know His love.

Here you are in the last part of this book. Hurrah for you! By now you understand that to show your love for God you must obey His commandments. He knows you and has made it simple by summarizing all the other commandments basically into the two we have concentrated on in this book and recorded in Matthew 22:37–39. They are not suggestions but are God's commandments. To not keep them is to be disobedient. To obey them is to show your love for God and to walk in the abundant blessings of His kingdom. Everything that any of the prophets or the law could say in the Old and New Testaments is here in these two commandments. It all comes out of love. That is why God has made known to you that no matter what you do, if it is not done with His love, it does not amount to anything (1 Cor. 13:1–3). Always remember, we love Him because He first loved us.

If you want to experience having your love needs met, if you want your love cup filled, you have to obey these two commandments. You must come to Him and yield yourself fully to Him (body, mind, soul, and strength) in love. When you do so, you will learn how to appreciate who you are and walk in freedom and love. Then you will be able to love others as you love yourself. Obeying these two commandments will set you apart from others in this world, for you will supernaturally be a vessel of Jesus Christ who *"receives"* and *"gives"* sincere divine love. Those outside of the family of God are operating in an imitation love that cannot fully satisfy. That is why it breaks my heart to see Christians abandon God's love for what the world has to offer. Look at the world! Look at the outcome of its relationships without God! Is the heartache and lack of commitment truly what anyone desires? Your very life can be the "love light" that opens their eyes and shows the way to this eternal agápe love.

God's ways are always the opposite of man's. There is so much teaching on being independent and sufficient in one's own abilities. Much encouragement is given to be strong by being an independent person. In contrast, in God's kingdom the more dependent you are upon Him the stronger you will be. *"Thus the children of Israel were brought under at that time, and the children of Judah prevailed, because they relied upon the Lord God of their fathers"* (2 Chron. 13:18, KJV). In God's kingdom, when you are your weakest, it is then that you are your strongest. *"Each time he said, 'My grace is all you need. My power works best in weakness.' So now I am glad to boast about my weaknesses, so that the power of Christ can work through me"* (2 Cor. 12:9, NLT).

It is in daily devotion and dependence upon Him that your "love light" gets brighter and brighter. The more time you spend in solitude with Jesus, the more you will get to know Him. As a matter of fact, you will become more Christlike. At salvation He clothed you in His robe of righteousness. This permitted you to have sweet fellowship with God. In sanctification, He teaches you to live out His righteousness in daily living. This permits you to have sweet fellowship with others. Although I cannot recall who said it, this person had a good point in regards to spending time with God. The person pointed out we do not "spend" time with God, because that denotes a loss. Instead we should view it as "investing" time, because that denotes a gain. We do not lose by investing time with Him.

This is why you will not hate yourself but learn to appreciate yourself. For you will be hid in Christ (Col. 3:3). It will be His thoughts, words, attitudes, and actions in you that will be observed and appreciated. Your delight is in Him, for the Holy Spirit has taken control of "self." Your devotion to Him is transforming you more and more into Christlikeness. This is what you are joyful over; this is what you are continuously giving thanks for! *"Instead, we will speak the truth in love, growing in every way more and more like Christ, who is the head of his body, the church"* (Eph. 4:15, NLT).

He will open your eyes to truth about yourself, others, and each area of your life. As you take one step at a time to obey what He says to you, you will be showing forth your love to Him. It is in losing yourself to Him completely that you will find yourself. You will stop despising how He made you and His plans for you. You will begin to confidently trust Him in all His decisions. You will thank Him for how uniquely He has made you and how He is fulfilling His call in your life. For example, you understand He gives many the gift of teaching. However, the style of your teaching may be different from someone else's. Through His love, you will learn to appreciate your own style in addition to that of others. There is no competition but oneness of Spirit. This is one way to learn how to love others as yourself.

At the same time, should you lack devotion in spending time with Him, your "love light" will become dim. You will not confidently trust Him or His dealings in your life. You will not become acquainted with His ways. The fleshly self will dominate, and you will be less Christlike. More than likely, you will have a distorted love for yourself and others. You will try to be like or better than others. There will not be oneness of Spirit, and you will not appreciate others excelling over yourself. *"This is what the Sovereign Lord, the Holy One of Israel, says: 'Only in returning to me and resting in me will you be saved. In quietness and confidence is your strength.' But you would have none of it"* (Isa. 30:15, NLT).

As a by-product of devotion and becoming more like Christ, His love will overflow from your heart to the heart of others. In seeking Him first, others will come in contact with a better you. For it will not be you at all, but Christ. He is your source of life and love. It is when you do not seek Him first that you will be functioning out of your own flesh when in contact with others. So, it is always beneficial to those who come in contact with you throughout each day when you carve out time to be with your Lord. You will be a better wife, mother, daughter, employee, friend, etc. You will see it is not a waste of time to put Him first. Yet your motivation should never be to put Christ first so you can have what you want with others. This is a distorted view. By making a decision to become fully devoted to Him, you will truly learn what life is about—that which is seen and unseen. *"Thou wilt shew me the path of life: In thy presence is fullness of joy; at thy right hand there are pleasures for evermore"* (Ps. 16:11, KJV). When you are devoted to Him, you will walk in His light and not stumble. When you are not devoted to Him, you will walk in darkness and not only stumble but fall. You are not here for temporal but eternal purposes. Your relationship with Jesus is a blessed privilege, not to be taken for granted. *"For God saved us and called us to live a holy life. He did this, not because we deserved it, but because that was his plan from before the beginning of time—to show us his grace through Christ Jesus"* (2 Tim. 1:9, NLT).

Deflection takes place when you turn aside or get off course or allow obstacles to hinder you. Your flesh, the devil, and the world constantly work to dim your light and keep you off course. You are going to have to put up a fight to not be deflected from your devotion to God. *"You neglected the Rock who had fathered you; you forgot the God who had given you birth"* (Deut. 32:18, NLT). There are so many Christians who have good intentions regarding having quiet time with God but who never get around to consistently doing it. How would you feel if you told your child to do something, and he or she always had an excuse as to why it could not be done? How would that make you feel as a parent? "I know you want me to go to bed right now, Mom, but I have to get so and so done. I will go to bed as soon as I can." Would that be acceptable to you as a parent? Then why do you feel that is acceptable to our heavenly Father? Jacob woke up after His encounter with God and said, "Surely the Lord was in this place, and I was not aware of it. (Gen. 28:11–16) This will be true for you if you allow yourself to be deflected from your devotions each day. Matthew 5:16 (KJV) instructs us, *"Let your light so shine before men, that they may see your good works, and glorify your Father which is in heaven."* What does it take to not be deflected from your devotion? You will need to maintain four simple steps: plan, pray, pursue, and persevere.

"By his divine power, God has given us everything we need for living a godly life. We have received all of this by coming to know him, the one who called us to himself by means of his marvelous glory and excellence. And because of his glory and excellence, he has given us great and precious promises. These are the promises that enable you to share his divine nature and escape the world's corruption caused by human desires. In view of all this, make every effort to respond to God's promises. Supplement your faith with a generous provision of moral excellence, and moral excellence with knowledge, and knowledge with self-control, and self-control with patient endurance, and patient endurance with godliness, and godliness with brotherly affection, and brotherly affection with love for everyone. The more you grow like this, the more productive and useful you will be in your knowledge of our Lord Jesus Christ. But those who fail to develop in this way are shortsighted or blind, forgetting that they have been cleansed from their old sins. So, dear brothers and sisters, work hard to prove that you really are among those God has called and chosen. Do these things, and you will never fall away" (2 Pet. 1:3–10, NLT).

Plan:

"Very early in the morning, while it was still dark, Jesus got up, left the house and went off to a solitary place, where he prayed" (Mark 1:35, NIV).

1. Prayerfully decide on a time for your devotions. Morning is best, but the main thing is to set time aside. Some of us are early birds and some are night owls. It is great to start your day with Jesus. Somehow miraculously, in a way I cannot explain, He makes the rest of the day fall into place. He orders your steps and clears your pathway when you seek Him first. *"But seek first the kingdom of God and His righteousness, and all these things shall be added to you"* (Matt. 6:33, NKJV). This is why you cannot afford to skip this time. It does not mean He removes all challenges or pain; that is a part of growth, but you will see Him redeem your time in a way that is unexplainable. You will learn to rest in Him, because you will trust that the way things are unfolding is in accordance with His plan. You will come to see that His plan for you is always good regardless of the present circumstances. You will be more sensitive to His interacting with you each day. For the night owls, you will have digested His Word before closing your eyes in

sleep. I like what Psalm 63:3–6 (KJV) states, *"Because thy lovingkindness is better than life, my lips shall praise thee. Thus will I bless thee while I live: I will lift up my hands in thy name. My soul shall be satisfied as with marrow and fatness; and my mouth shall praise thee with joyful lips: When I remember thee upon my bed, and meditate on thee in the night watches."*

2. Decide on a place. It is a holy place, where you will meet with Jesus each day. It should be a place of solitude away from distractions. As you develop a discipline in meeting Jesus here each day, it will become a very special place.

3. Decide on your devotional material. The one and only thing you really need is the Bible. I suggest you use a study Bible and not a paraphrase, such as *The Message*. You can use paraphrases when just reading at another time. However, if it helps, you may want to have these items as well: a devotional book (which has suggested Bible reading for each day), markers or pens (to make notes or to highlight words, sentences, etc. in your Bible), notebook or journal (to write what you have learned), Bible study materials (Bible dictionaries, commentaries, workbooks, etc.). A host of electronic Bible study materials can make it very easy to study without having volumes of books spread out on a desk or table. Now you can view them on the computer (even at our website), on your cell phone, on iPods, and on other electronic devices. You can have readily available volumes of study material to help you in your quest to know Jesus better. The main thing is to have a place for everything and everything in its place. This will help you not to be distracted in your devotional time.

4. Decide on a plan in case of emergencies. Should you have an emergency that calls you away from your set time with Jesus, you may want to have a small Bible that fits into your pocketbook or car. Then if time allows, you can at least read some Scriptures and pray. It may comfort you to have the Word right there to minister during a crisis—the Psalms bring great comfort. Remember God is love. Do not feel condemned when you have to miss your devotional time. You may start off with this routine being a duty and one of obedience. However, it should not remain that way.

After spending time with Jesus, it should move from duty to delight, where you cannot wait to meet with Him. This comes as you are consistently meeting with Him. It will get to a point you do not want to miss this time, not because of shame and guilt but because of loss of fellowship and communion with Him.

Pray:

"Do not be anxious about anything, but in everything, by prayer and petition, with thanksgiving, present your requests to God. And the peace of God, which transcends all understanding, will guard your hearts and your minds in Christ Jesus" (Phil. 4:6–7, NIV).

1. Prayer is nothing to be afraid of. You are entering the presence of a Holy Father who loves you and who has proven it by sending His Son on your behalf. It is talking to Him openly and honestly. It does not benefit to try to hide anything from Him, because He knows all things and still desires to fellowship with you.
2. You first ask Him to open your spiritual eyes and ears that you may see and hear Him as you read His Word. Acknowledge anything He shows you, and thank Him for His guidance and forgiveness where you may have strayed in your fellowship with Him.
3. Prayer is not just entering into His presence, and you doing all the talking. Prayer is two-way communication with God. Take time to be quiet and listen. Let Him talk to you through His indwelling Spirit and His Word. See if He puts something on your heart. If so, then be obedient to do as He has directed you. Write down what He puts on your heart so you do not forget it.
4. It is showing deep respect to be on your knees when you pray. Having a soft pillow may cushion your knee joints. Of course, you will find times when you will pray in all positions: standing, walking, etc. Prayer can be open where others may hear your words, but at times you may pray silently, when only Jesus hears you. This is your special place to become intimate with your Savior. Intimate friends

share everything and know they will not be judged. Jesus is your true intimate friend. Pour out your heart to Him.
5. Prayer is an expression of your devotion and dependence upon God. You do not want to proceed to do anything without getting His insight into the situation or decision. It is honoring Him to seek his wisdom above your own before you start your day and all throughout the day as you go about your tasks. At the conclusion of your day, give thanks for all that He has done.

Pursue:

"Ever since I first heard of your strong faith in the Lord Jesus and your love for God's people everywhere, I have not stopped thanking God for you. I pray for you constantly, asking God, the glorious Father of our Lord Jesus Christ, to give you spiritual wisdom and insight so that you might grow in your knowledge of God. I pray that your hearts will be flooded with light so that you can understand the confident hope he has given to those he called—his holy people who are his rich and glorious inheritance. I also pray that you will understand the incredible greatness of God's power for us who believe him. This is the same mighty power that raised Christ from the dead and seated him in the place of honor at God's right hand in the heavenly realms. Now he is far above any ruler or authority or power or leader or anything else—not only in this world but also in the world to come. God has put all things under the authority of Christ and has made him head over all things for the benefit of the church. And the church is his body; it is made full and complete by Christ, who fills all things everywhere with himself" (Eph. 1:15–23, NLT).

1. Once you have your designated place and all your materials, and you have started your time alone with Him in prayer, the next thing you want to do is read His Word. He reveals Himself to you through His Word. The more you learn about Jesus, the more you will learn about the Father. The Father is revealed in the Son (John 1:14; 14:9). It is through His Word that you will commune further with God. He will show you everything you need to know: His will, His promises, His forgiveness, His provision, His desire for your life, His view on love [examples to follow], sins to forsake, stumbling blocks to avoid, etc. There is nothing in this life

you need that is not addressed in God's Word. If it is not spelled out in black and white, there will be a principle to guide you into His truth.
2. The whole objective of having a quiet time with Jesus is to get to *know Him*. It is not to boast of what you know about the Scriptures or that you read it from cover to cover each year. The whole objective of your Christian walk is not to **do** ministry, but to get to **know** Him. This is the goal not just on Sunday but every moment of your life. This does not mean you are carrying the Bible around with you, but you are conscious of Jesus's presence with you at all times. So you are anticipating Him every moment to lead, guide, instruct, encourage, and give insight to you. Of course, He does this through His Word, but He will do it in many ways through His indwelling Spirit within you, through people, nature, circumstances, etc. You must be alert and sensitive to how He speaks to you throughout the day. This is the tantalizing experience of the Christian each day—to walk with Jesus along the way—just like Adam and Eve. It is your private delight and pleasure. You pursue *Him* in all things. *"And we know that the Son of God has come and has given us an understanding, that we may know Him who is true; and we are in Him who is true, in His Son Jesus Christ. This is the true God and eternal life"* (1 John 5:20, NKJV).
3. As you read His Word, learn to pray back to Him what is stated in His Word (promises, His words regarding you, precious insights on how to conduct yourself, etc.).
4. Always try to learn at least one thing about God each time you sit quietly with Him. Ask the three questions used in inductive Bible study each time you read God's Word:
    a. What does it say? [What is God saying in His Word?]
    b. What does it mean? [What are the facts presented—geography, original setting, and word meanings? Observe as many details as possible.]
    c. What does it mean to me? [What are the sins to forsake, promises to claim, commands to obey, examples to follow, and errors to avoid?]

5. By faith, put into practice what you have learned, even if it is to just trust Him more.
6. His Word will become a mirror revealing the truth about who you are: your desires, motives, and expectations. Jot down everything He is teaching you so you will not just be a hearer of His Word, but a doer (James 1:22).
7. Thank Him for who He is and what you have learned at the end of your time together.
8. Reading His Word is a must. Learning to meditate on His Word (reflecting over and over again to get deeper understanding for you personally) and to memorize (commit His Word to your heart so you can bring it to mind without the written Bible) are important too. In addition, participate in a Bible study that digs even deeper than your quiet time allows.
9. Your entire life is affected by reading the Word. Christians are to live by faith (2 Cor. 5:7). Well, faith comes by hearing the Word (Rom. 10:17). Faith is a confident trust in God. You will not have a confident trust in God without knowing Him through His Word. The Holy Spirit directs through the Word to reveal whether you are operating under the control of your flesh or the Spirit. You will live your life predominately under the control of one or the other. The price you pay for living according to the flesh is very costly, but people do not make the connection between their misery and the lack of God's Word in their lives. They easily blame other people, organizations, or circumstances, all the time not seeing they are the ones who have put the nail in their own coffins. Oh, that our eyes would be open to see this connection and to cry out to God for help in not neglecting His Word! Please pursue Him with all your heart.

Persevere:

"Do not merely listen to the word, and so deceive yourselves. Do what it says. Anyone who listens to the word but does not do what it says is like a man who looks at his face in a mirror and, after looking at himself, goes away and immediately forgets what he looks like. But the man who looks intently

into the perfect law that gives freedom, and continues to do this, not forgetting what he has heard, but doing it—he will be blessed in what he does" (James 1:22–25, NIV).

1. As you sit before the Lord, He is transforming you into His likeness. You are becoming holy as He is holy. Holiness has to do with being set apart. As you become more like Christ you are set apart from the world (its mind-set, desires, passions, etc.) for His glory. For this very reason, Satan will set out to destroy you (John 10:10). He will oppose every step you make to draw closer to God, which is why you must persevere and be determined to stay close to God.
2. Give Jesus your total focus and attention. There is nothing more important at this time. When your mind wanders, ask the Lord to return it to Him and to help you concentrate on Him only. Do not be preoccupied with other things at the same time.
3. You will have a peace and faith during your trials that does not make sense. You will experience His keeping you in sickness, disappointments, and all of life's struggles. His peace passes all understanding (Phil. 4:7).
4. You can relinquish control. You do not need to manipulate, compete, or make demands. You know God is in control, and you leave the consequences of your faith and obedience to Him.
5. You will learn to keep your eyes on Him so He may guide, direct, protect, and provide.
6. You will experience the freedom Jesus purchased for you on the cross. You will no longer need masks, facades, or appearances before others. You can be authentic, not hypocritical—showing one lifestyle in the open while hiding another lifestyle behind the scenes. You understand that your personal worth is not determined by your works but by what Christ did for you on the cross.
7. You will recognize your way of escape when temptation afflicts you (1 Cor. 10:13).
8. You will be used of God to accomplish His will on earth in the power of His strength through the Holy Spirit. Isn't it wonderful that you do not have to depend upon your own

strength when persevering? *"So do not fear, for I am with you; do not be dismayed, for I am your God. I will strengthen you and help you; I will uphold you with my righteous right hand"* (Isa. 41:10, NIV).

Do not let your devotional time become monotonous or just a duty. Here are some things others have tried during their devotional time:

1. Use a different translation annually,
2. Fast from food in addition to devotion to prayer and study for a certain number of hours,
3. Keep a journal of what you are learning from His Word for that year and reflect back on it often to strengthen your faith,
4. Try various types of devotional books and material to gain new insight each year,
5. One woman said she plays real soft music while sitting quietly before the Lord. [Depending on your personality, you may find absolute quiet a detriment to your devotion time. Of course, your music should be without lyrics so you can concentrate on hearing God's Words. Music for other personalities would be a distraction. Isn't it great how we are all made differently?]
6. Teach your children to respect your time with Jesus. [Let them know you are not to be disturbed unless it is an emergency. Repeatedly stand firm on their having patience and waiting until you are done. This will demonstrate to them the importance of spending time with God as they mature. If you know your children are early birds, you may need to have cereal or the toy for the crib ready just in case they call during this time. Be creative and ask the Lord to give you insight on how to deal with small children so as not to be torn away from your devotional time. The better thing to do, if you are able, is to get up early before they rise or wait until they are down for bed to have your time.]

Find out what works for you and be consistent and diligent in spending time with Him. Consistency is the key. A time will come when you will not want to miss it, and you will begin to spend even more time

Dropped but Not Broken

with Him than when you started. So start out small, reading a little, and then move on to a greater portion of Scripture and prayer each day. The time with Him will be precious and fulfilling. Pray before and after for the Holy Spirit to give you insight, for without Him, you will not grasp what God has to say to you personally.

Jesus is fully devoted to you in every aspect of your life. Please keep the same mind-set about Him. You will not regret it if you plan, pray, pursue, and persevere in your devotion to Him. You cannot have a passion for Christ and a passion for the world at the same time. *"This is the message we have heard from him and declare to you: God is light; in him there is no darkness at all. If we claim to have fellowship with him yet walk in the darkness, we lie and do not live by the truth. But if we walk in the light, as he is in the light, we have fellowship with one another, and the blood of Jesus, his Son, purifies us from all sin"* (1 John 1:5–7, NIV).

If you are consistent with your devoted quiet time with Him, you will see Jesus. You will learn to love Him with all of your heart, mind, soul, and strength. Your love for Him will increase and manifold blessings will unfold that you will want everyone to experience. Deflection from devotion to your Savior will take place if you allow yourself to be deceived or distracted by other things that appear to be more urgent than this vital time with your Lord. Make a commitment now not to let that happen. Once again, if something happens out of your control, do not beat yourself up but pick right back up as quickly as you can. *"But you, dear friends, build yourselves up in your most holy faith and pray in the Holy Spirit. Keep yourselves in God's love as you wait for the mercy of our Lord Jesus Christ to bring you to eternal life"* (Jude 20–21, NIV).

There is a quote by Woody Guthrie (the songwriter who wrote "This Land Is Your Land"), which states, "Seeking the aid of the Holy Spirit, let us aim at perfection. Let every day see some sin crucified, some battle fought, some good done, some victory won; let every fall be followed by a rise, and every step gained become, not a resting-place, but a new starting-point for further and higher progress."[5] Sarah Young (who wrote *Jesus Calling*) expressed how this unmeasurable and vast ocean of love cannot be measured or explained, but how it can be experienced.[6] This will be your personal experience as you learn to love without limits.

Love without Limits

Yvonne somehow had an inner peace when the elevator doors closed. She was going to the third floor to meet her daughter. It was the second time she had been admitted to this rehab for anorexia. Yvonne put her faith in God concerning her daughter, and God had continuously provided her the strength to hold on. Oh, there were tears and times she thought she could not take another step with her daughter, but God would intervene each time. It seemed the more she tried to love her, the more her daughter would push her away. What would happen this time when she came home? The elevator doors opened, and Yvonne stepped out and smiled when she saw her daughter waiting by the door.

In letting your "love light" shine, you realize you must devote some time each day with Jesus. As mandatory as this is, you must come out of the secret place with Him to live among others. This is where it is easy for your light to dim. Your relationships in your home, family, church, and community must be maintained with this holy love light. This is easier said than done. To declare that you are all right just having a relationship with Jesus and not being bothered with the rest is to stop short of God's design for you in *receiving* and *giving* love. Even if your heart has been torn into pieces, it is important to love without limits. This does not mean you allow yourself to be abused or misused. To love without limits is to entrust your security and protection to God while you love others unconditionally. It means you are not going to place certain conditions on your love for others—they do not have to meet certain criteria to be loved by you. You recognized that you are stepping into a relationship as a representative of Jesus. You will love others in the same way He would have loved them. Your love is not dependent upon people and their actions, regardless of your past mistakes or hurts caused by others. You do not have to give up on love. Listen to that … to give up on love is to give up on God. You know the reason why—God is love. All is not lost. Love can be restored in your life. Of course, Matthew 22:37–40 and 1 John 3:23 are the motivations for loving without limits.

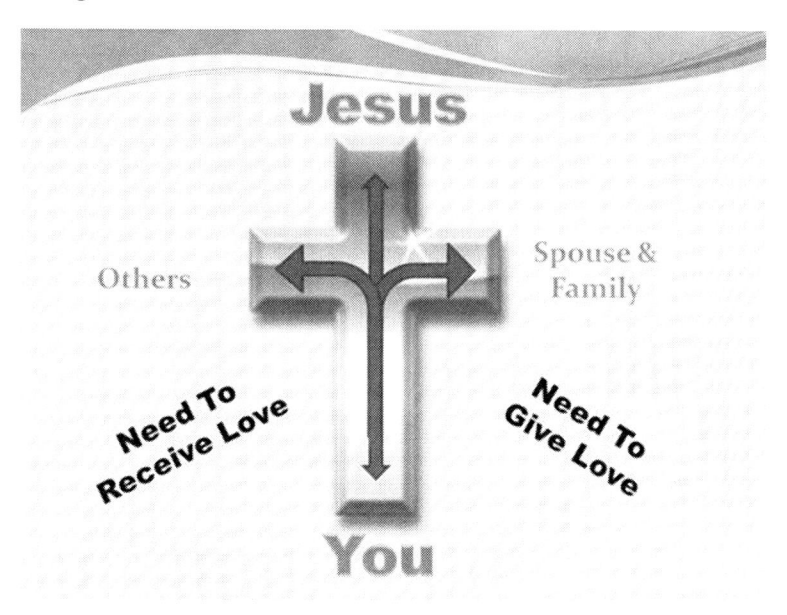

First John 4:16–17 (NIV) states, *"And so we know and rely on the love God has for us. God is love. Whoever lives in love lives in God, and God in him. In this way, love is made complete among us so that we will have confidence on the Day of Judgment, because in this world we are like him."* Looking at the illustration, God's love is made complete as love flows between Jesus and you, and then between you and others. Jesus fulfills the need you have to *receive* and then *give* love. It is a love that flows from the inside out. Jesus's love flows down to you, and then this love flows back to Him and then to others.

The Gospel of John records something that is important for us to remember when dealing with others. Judas was about to betray Jesus. This is what Jesus said in John 14:30–31 (KJV), *"Hereafter I will not talk much with you: for the prince of this world cometh, and hath nothing in me. But that the world may know that I love the Father; and as the Father gave me commandment, even so I do. Arise, let us go hence."* Note the words of Jesus, "The prince of this world cometh, and hath nothing in Me." The prince of this world is Satan. How was Satan coming? Satan was coming through the conduct of Judas. He had nothing in Jesus, but the same could not be said of Judas. You could say Satan did have power, influence, or fellowship with Judas. The reason why he had this on Judas was because Judas gave in to temptation and sinned when he decided to betray Jesus. More could be said on this, but I do not want you to lose the train of thought. So Satan had something on Judas because he sinned. You can almost picture a hook in Judas because he sinned. By having a hook in Judas, Satan could pull and lead him in the direction that he pleased. Just like you can pull and direct a fish once you have a hook in him. This is important to remember.

In contrast, Jesus said Satan did not have anything in Him. Jesus was the sinless Son of God. Unlike Judas, Satan did not have a hook in Him. Satan had no part in Jesus. Satan did not influence His behavior at all. He had no fellowship with Him either. Furthermore, Satan did not have power over Jesus. (Jesus would voluntarily yield to the death of the cross in loving obedience to the Father. Satan did not make him go to the cross. Read the passage again.)

Look at another incident in Scripture where Satan influenced the behavior of an individual. *"And He began to teach them that the Son of Man must suffer many things, and be rejected by the elders and chief priests and scribes, and be killed, and after three days rise again. He spoke this word openly. Then Peter took Him aside and began to rebuke Him. But when He had turned around and looked at His disciples, He rebuked Peter, saying, 'Get behind Me, Satan! For you are not mindful of the things of God, but the things of men'"* (Mark 8:31–33, NKJV). In this incident, Peter had a "hook" in him. In other words, Satan was influencing his thoughts and words—he was rebuking Jesus! Jesus addressed Satan directly when He spoke to Peter. Again, Satan had nothing in Jesus, but the same could not be said of Peter at this time.

Now to be fair, Jesus is the only sinless man that walked on this earth. We know we have sinned, as stated in Romans 5:12 (NLT), *"When Adam sinned, sin entered the world. Adam's sin brought death, so death spread to everyone, for everyone sinned."* Even though as a Christian your sins will never be held against you because of Jesus's substitutionary death for you, sin is still in this world. As sure as you are a human being who breathes every day, you will encounter sin in this world until Jesus comes back. This sin brings about conflicts in your relationships (divorce, offenses, arguments, murder, abuse, hurts, separation, etc.).

Satan comes in through the conduct of people in relationships. The thing that needs to be learned from this passage is to live in a way that does not allow the enemy to put a hook in you. Live so you do not by sinning permit him fellowship, influence, or power over your behavior. He should have *nothing in you*. Now stay with me so you can gain understanding on this. Don't turn me off.

Of course, a Christian cannot be demon possessed. A Christian is the holy temple of God (1 Cor. 3:17) and cannot house the Holy Spirit of God and an evil demon at the same time (2 Cor. 6:15–16). It is not like the days of Judas and Peter, when the Holy Spirit only came *upon* people to accomplish a task. It was not until the victory was won by Jesus's death and resurrection that the Holy Spirit came to abide always *within* believers. This permanent filling of the Holy Spirit first took place on the Day of Pentecost (Acts, chap. 2). However, Satan and his demons can oppress Christians today. He can influence you through tempting you by your own flesh, the world, and His schemes to sin (Eph. 2:1–3).

The goal is not to give Satan a place in your life by yielding to sin. To do so would be to walk out of the light of God's fellowship into the darkness of the world (Satan's domain). This would be the same as allowing him to place a hook in you and influence your conduct. It would be the same as having fellowship with, being under the influence of, or allowing him to have power over your behavior. Just as Satan had nothing in Jesus because He was perfectly sinless (holy), you should passionately purpose to live a holy life as well (1 Pet. 1:15). Satan had no power over Jesus, and He does not have power over you unless you yield to him. You have to give him permission. *"You are of God, little children, and have overcome them, because He who is in you is greater than he who is in the world"* (1 John 4:4, NKJV). Jesus, who is in you, is greater than Satan, who is in the world.

Here are a few ways a Christian may give place to the devil (there are more):

1. *"And don't sin by letting anger control you. Don't let the sun go down while you are still angry, for anger gives a foothold to the devil"* (Eph. 4:26–27, NLT).
2. *"Satan replied to the Lord, 'Skin for skin! A man will give up everything he has to save his life. But reach out and take away*

his health, and he will surely curse you to your face'" (Job 2:4–5, NLT)!
3. *"Do not love this world nor the things it offers you, for when you love the world, you do not have the love of the Father in you. For the world offers only a craving for physical pleasure, a craving for everything we see, and pride in our achievements and possessions. These are not from the Father, but are from this world. And this world is fading away, along with everything that people crave. But anyone who does what pleases God will live forever"* (1 John 2:15–17, NLT).
4. *"But people who long to be rich fall into temptation and are trapped by many foolish and harmful desires that plunge them into ruin and destruction. For the love of money is the root of all kinds of evil. And some people, craving money, have wandered from the true faith and pierced themselves with many sorrows"* (1 Tim. 6:9–10, NLT).

So Satan can tempt you to sin, but he cannot make you sin. That is a willful choice that you make. Giving in to temptation starts by allowing a good desire to get out of control. If this desire is not brought under the control of the Holy Spirit, you will give place or control to Satan. Then here comes the hook! Remember, he should have *nothing in you*. I use the hook to give you an illustration to keep in mind when yielding to temptation, which is sin. Here are a few things to remember about temptation as well:

1. There is not one Christian who has not been tempted. It is commonplace to all. Just because you are tempted, does not mean you have sinned. Jesus was tempted, and He is without sin. Again, everyone is tempted, but the sin does not occur until you give in to the temptation. It is only when you go ahead and involve yourself in the temptation that sin has taken place.
2. Sin is a willful decision to give in to temptation. *"The temptations in your life are no different from what others experience. And God is faithful. He will not allow the temptation to be more than you can stand. When you are tempted, he will show you a way out so that you can endure"* (1 Cor. 10:13,

NLT). So there is a promise from God that He will always provide a way for you to escape temptation. The only thing is, you must be willing to see your escape and take it. It's there! It is your choice: God's way or Satan's way. That is it. One will lead to life, and the other will lead to death (separation). As a Christian you are not talking about your eternal life being taken away, but your sweet fellowship will be hindered. Sin will break your fellowship with a Holy God. This is the separation (death) that will take place. It is not worth it; don't give in to the temptation. Although you may be surprised by the magnitude of the temptation and its destruction, God never is. He is omniscient and sees all things. That is how He is always able to provide an escape for you right on time. Second Peter 2:9 also confirms that God is able to deliver the godly out of temptation.

3. The source of your temptation is the devil (see the temptation of Jesus in Matthew 4:1–11). God is not the source of anything that would cause you to fall away from Him (James 1:13). However, God will allow you to face temptation so that you may face it, overcome it in His strength, and become stronger in your Christian walk (see Job 1:6–12). His allowance is always for your good, not for your destruction. *"Blessed is the man that endureth temptation: for when he is tried, he shall receive the crown of life, which the Lord hath promised to them that love him"* (James 1:12, KJV). That is why He is faithful to always provide a way out for you. Satan's purpose is always for your destruction. Satan *tempts* for evil purposes; God *allows* for good purposes.

4. Temptation begins in your mind with a desire. The desire spins out of control until you commit some act of sin. *"Temptation comes from our own desires, which entice us and drag us away. These desires give birth to sinful actions. And when sin is allowed to grow, it gives birth to death"* (James 1:14–15, NLT). Satan would have you believe that if you strongly desire something, you may as well go ahead and do it because you have already sinned. No matter how strong your flesh may cry out, if you resist you will have been obedient to God. Satan may convince you that one time is not wrong either. Billy Graham says, "None of us should deliberately place

ourselves in a position to be tempted. Satan will always attack where we are the most vulnerable." This is how it is normally played out: you get an evil thought, and you dwell on it; it festers and grows (sometimes multiplying into more evil thoughts and attitudes), and then you carry out an evil act of sin.
5. Dr. Charles Stanley warns it is easier to give in to temptation when you are physically tired, hungry, or lonely. This is so true. Other times of temptation may come easily when you have periods of idleness, are under emotional stress, are fearful or anxious, or even at times of blessings (tempted to become prideful).
6. Being tempted does not necessarily mean you are weak. It could be a sign of being strong. The stronger you are as a Christian who resists temptation, the more of a threat you are to Satan. You will be a strong warrior for the Kingdom of God by consistently overcoming when tempted. The Lord rejoices over you while the enemy is upset about you. As you become stronger, turn around and strengthen others. *"Simon, Simon, Satan has asked to sift each of you like wheat. But I have pleaded in prayer for you, Simon, that your faith should not fail. So when you have repented and turned to me again, strengthen your brothers"* (Luke 22:31–32, NLT).

To love without limits is to be as Jesus—let Satan have nothing in you. Satan will try over and over again to defeat you, but walk in such obedience to the Lord that he cannot gain any ground in your life. The more you resist Satan, the stronger you will become. *"Don't be misled—you cannot mock the justice of God. You will always harvest what you plant. Those who live only to satisfy their own sinful nature will harvest decay and death from that sinful nature. But those who live to please the Spirit will harvest everlasting life from the Spirit. So let's not get tired of doing what is good. At just the right time we will reap a harvest of blessing if we don't give up. Therefore, whenever we have the opportunity, we should do good to everyone—especially to those in the family of faith"* (Gal. 6:7–10, NLT).

Decide now to love without limits in accordance with what you have learned from God's Word. By doing so you will be able to love from the inside out in a way others who are without Jesus cannot possibly do. You will also love in a way that is contrary to the world. Be careful to not compromise. To compromise means to give in to your flesh, the world, and Satan. Compromise is cooperating with what is against God's commandments for love. For example: to live with someone of the opposite sex without being married, to match yourself up with an unsaved person, to commit fornication or adultery, to take advice more from worldly magazines on how to love another over what God says in His Word, to use another person for your own selfish needs, etc. Even as a Christian you may reason—everyone lives this way! Especially as more and more scandals are released in the news about clergy, you may have lost all hope of living in accordance with what God says about love. The chaos in present-day relationships is a result of not believing God and of everyone doing their own thing. God established relationships. He is the one who can tell you how relationships work. Those who decide to love without limits will experience joy even in the midst of trials. *"Joyful are people of integrity, who follow the instructions of the Lord. Joyful are those who obey his laws and search for him with all their hearts. They do not compromise with evil, and they walk only in his paths"* (Ps. 119:1–3, NLT).

Whenever I lose my peace, I always ask God to reveal the cause and give me wisdom. "God, what is going on here? Why am I upset? Why am I irritated? Why am I starting to get angry?" You can start to learn how to discern whether you are operating in self or the Spirit. You can become sensitive as to whether you are operating with your own human love or His agápe love. God wants you to know, because he wants His love and peace to rule your heart. You really have to trust and come to Him for this. You will need to deny yourself, take up your cross, and follow him.

John 21:17–22 (NKJV) says, *"He said to him, the third time, 'Simon, son of Jonah, do you love me?' And Peter was grieved because he said to him the third time, 'Do you love me?' And he said to him, 'Lord, you know all things. You know that I love you.' And Jesus said to him, 'Feed my sheep. Most assuredly, I say to you, when you were younger, you girded yourself and walked where you wished, but when you were old, you will stretch out your hands and another will gird you and carry you where you do not wish.' This he spoke, signifying of what death he would glorify God. And when he had spoken this,* he said to him, 'follow me.' Then Peter, turning around, saw the disciple, whom Jesus loved which was John, following, who also had leaned on his breast at the supper and said, 'Lord, who is the one who betrayed you?' Peter seeing him says to Jesus, 'But Lord, what about this man?' And Jesus said to him, 'If I will that he remains until I come, what is that to you? Follow me.'" So here, Jesus is saying, "Peter, do you love me?" And Peter answers, "Yes, Lord, you know I love you." Jesus comes back and questions him again. Peter gets frustrated. He does not realize Jesus is pointing out to him that, "Yes, you love me, but it's not with My agápe love. It's with your own natural human love. I want you to come onto the level of My agápe love."

To love without limits is to love on this level of agápe love that Jesus is talking about. When you love on this level you will not be concerned primarily about what the other person is doing (as Peter was with John), but you will concentrate on your obedience to Christ. What I mean by this is that you are going to do what He has said even if no one else does so. So in regards to loving without limits, your concentration is on His words, "Follow Me." It is enough for you to make sure you are following Christ.

When your brother and sister fall or they are not meeting your desires or they are not meeting your expectations, what you have to do in love is allow them to grow. You should turn them over to the Lord, and let the Lord in His love and in His time draw them and help them. You have enough to deal with in your love walk, so just continue to give them love and wait on God. I am not saying you do not step in and help others. I am saying you do not try to govern or control everyone else's life according to your expectations. That is what I am learning. Let go of others having to meet your expectations. You have enough in dealing with yourself. For you to start trying to tell another what you think should be done is taking on the work of the Holy Spirit. Too much time is wasted on such behavior and does not build strong relationships. Additionally, do not let others treat you in this manner. When you live this way, you will walk in freedom. Remember, Jesus replied, "What is that to you? Do what I told you to do."

People in this world today need to see Jesus's love, and we are not the light and salt we used to be as the body of Christ. By not operating in His love, what is happening? Our families are being destroyed. Our marriages are no different than those of unbelievers. Friendships even in the Christian church are affected by one person backstabbing another. It is a result of operating in your own natural love. Come up onto the level of agápe love.

You want to know how to *receive* and to *give* love? Open yourself up to God's plan regarding love and relationships. As much as others may want to satisfy you, they cannot do so for your entire life. Additionally, you will frustrate them by trying to make them meet your desires and needs. Only God can do that. So when they do meet a need in some way, it is like peanut butter in the Reese's cup—it is an extra delight. Here we go with the food again. The bottom line is to trust God with your needs.

I believe God has allowed me to go through some things in getting this book together, and I have felt self saying, "Don't you dare share that. Don't you dare say anything about that." However, God's Spirit was saying, "Paula, trust Me. I allowed you to experience some things so you would share, because I'm going to have hurting women read this material. This is not about you. This is about My using you so I may get the glory." So I wanted to share some of my own selfishness, and I pray it will help you and will lift you up. May you see you should never, never exalt anyone above the Lord. I will share examples from my life regarding the three areas of relationships: spouse, family, and friends.

In regards to my spouse and hubby for many years, he too was given freedom of choice by God. In exercising his freedom, he made some choices that really ended up hurting our relationship. At two different times, there were women who entered his life and tried to break up our marriage. My husband did not act the way I desired, nor did he handle it as quickly as I desired. Therefore, I had a lot of hurt. I have his permission to share this so you may be helped by our story.

With the first woman, I had a lot of anger and fight in me. Self was all about protecting what was mine (self-preservation). I really do believe had God not kept me in His love, I would have done something that I would have regretted.

When the second woman came with the purpose of destroying our marriage, I had grown in the love of God, and I found myself operating in His agápe love this time. I was indeed hurt and upset over how my hubby handled things, but this time I relied totally upon God's love of me to protect me from harm and to deal with William. I cannot explain it, but He gave me strength to conduct myself in a godly manner and to not operate in my flesh. There was a grave difference in how I conducted myself the first time and the next time. Furthermore, I was able to let God deal with William. He had a choice himself—whether he was going to operate in self or whether he was going to do what God would have him to do.

I set up necessary boundaries with him, but I dealt with Paula. I drew nigh to God as He instructed in His Word, and I found He drew nigh to me. I said, "Okay, Father. You've always had my back. I know You have it now. You just show me what You want me to do. I trust you to work in William's heart as well." Do you know that God will fight your battles? Do you know that God will protect you? As the psalmist said in Psalm 46, *"Even though the mountains give way and fall into the sea."* You must be persuaded in your own heart of God's love for you. When you are, it does not matter what happens with the circumstances. You know by faith God is going to protect you.

My eyes are not closed to reality. Being in women's ministry, I sometimes see husbands leave good women. Sad to say, it is happening in Christian homes all the time. That does not mean you are not a good woman or you have not been a good wife. It just means that your spouse had a choice, and he yielded to self and not to the Savior. You cannot stop him from doing so; it's his choice. So you have to deal with yourself before the Lord, and allow the Lord to fight your battles. You do not have to run around frantically checking cell phones. When you are walking with God and operating under the control of His Spirit, he will make things known to you. Whatever you need to know about those you have a relationship with, he will tell you. However, you must be operating in a love relationship with him every day to experience this for yourself. You cannot experience this by operating in self. God is faithful. What He reveals may crush you, because it comes out of the blue and hurts, but if you stay in the Spirit, and not operate in your own desires and flesh, you will witness God's mighty acts of love toward you. I am telling you the truth! He will instruct you as to what boundaries to set up and what actions to take in spite of him. He will show you how to send a strong message to your spouse that such behavior is not acceptable and will not be tolerated. When He is guiding in this way, there is an unexplainable peace and strength that you know is only coming from Him. You are not operating in anger or fretting or spewing off steam. The Spirit's moving is so much different from that of the flesh.

I can honestly say William and I have a stronger marriage because of the trials we had to overcome together. These two experiences took us from a lot of surface issues right down to the root of the problems. Like any marriage, though, we work on it continually. You cannot let your guard down at all. I don't care how good of a man you have. I have a good man, but there are young girls out there who want a sugar daddy. They do not really want to marry him, but they just want somebody to take them places and do things for them.

Having said that, let me give you another warning. It does not matter how happily married you are now; you need to take steps to maintain your marriage and not get complacent. Take care of your appearance as well. Go to Victoria's Secret or do something once in a while to spice things up. Are you thinking, "I cannot believe she told me, as a Christian woman, to go to Victoria's Secret!" Well, do something to keep excitement in your relationship. It may not thrill you, but it will indeed thrill him (smile).

If you are reading this and your husband has left you already, I am sorry. I am truly sorry. God's plan is for a man and a wife to stay together. Even if you are in a marriage with an unsaved husband, that house is sanctified because you have God's Spirit in you. What I mean by sanctified is your house is set apart. It is still something special about your house because God's Spirit is in it. God's agápe love can be displayed through you, so do not smother it, but let it work in your home. If you have an unsaved husband, and it's hard to deal with him and your children, still show them God's agápe love.

Face it, as a woman you have to manage many things. As a result, you may not realize you are being disrespectful to your husband by barking orders to him as if he was one of the kids. Do not be disrespectful. You may be good at multitasking, but you must be careful not to control your husband. I am sharing these things as the Lord puts them on my heart to spare you pain. The one thing a man needs is respect. If he does not have respect, he will find it somewhere else. I always try to show William respect even after what happened to us. The other major thing he needs is intimacy through sex. Oh my, that's a whole different book. You cannot say you love him and not give your body to him in this way. Physiologically, he truly does need sex. It is his makeup. So learn all you can about this area if that is a weakness in your marriage. I would recommend the book and video series entitled, *Love and Respect*, by Emerson Eggerichs.

Here is another example in regards to family relationships. My sons, when they became grown men, began to make decisions that were not to my liking. At times their choice of females had me praying, "Oh, God, get that woman out of his life." I remember this one girl who would give Dolly Parton competition (if you know what I mean). I thought, "All he sees are those." I prayed and prayed and prayed. When my son brought her to the house, it grieved me to see them together. I could not even see her face for the … you know. (Now this is not against any of you who are endowed by God in this area.)

Do you know we have got to let our children grow up? We have to stop giving our love and withholding it according to how they please us. Agápe love is unconditional. It is not only displayed when we are proud of them but when they displease us as well. God's love teaches you to be patient and bear with others as they grow and make mistakes. This is where your faith is tested over and over again. The more you understand how God treats you this way, the more you are able to do the same for others. This frees you from judging others and lets them grow and be led of God. As God bestows His grace upon you, you in turn bestow grace upon others. You will learn to guard your mouth, your thoughts, and your actions as you try to love someone this way.

This way of living is not easy at first and will make you miserable. I was miserable at times because their actions did not align with my expectations. I wanted to step in and tell them what they needed to do. I only share now when doors of opportunity are open. An example of this would be a mom hovering over her child like a helicopter. I never gave up praying as I waited upon the Lord to help them see His way. Manipulation and control are not options. You must trust God. The thrill I have now is to see how faithful God is in instructing them and having them come back and share the very same thing I wanted to say to them. It is exciting to see them being led of God.

I remember when I was preparing the lesson that was the foundation for this book, I had prayed, "Oh, Lord, reach my neighbors, save my neighbors. Let me, Father, be able to reach my neighbors for you." Oh, we can be so holy at times. I had an afternoon designated to work on this material and be quiet before the Lord. Everything was flowing nicely; it was all going as planned. Then all of a sudden, my neighbor across the street came over. Another neighbor had a loved one die, and this neighbor wanted me to try to help the other neighbor. I thought, "Oh, this is inconvenient." Who was I thinking about right then? Self.

Another time, I was working on a lesson, and my other neighbor came over and told me she was really sick and asked if I could take her to the doctor. At first, my flesh was screaming, "No, she did not come at this time wanting me to take her. Not when I'm on a roll again." Then the Spirit said, "Paula." I responded, "You are right, Lord. I prayed about this. I asked you if I could reach my neighbors." Although it took my entire afternoon to run her around, it was a great opportunity to talk with her.

In reading this I do not want you to place yourself under a load of condemnation because you realize how much you operate in your flesh as I have shared of my shortcomings. You may be thinking, "Gosh, I am in the flesh all the time. My Christianity isn't making any difference in my life." Romans 8:1 lets us know there is no condemnation to those who are in Christ Jesus who walk not after the flesh, but after the Spirit. You cannot stop the initial promptings of your flesh. This flesh is going to scream and say all kinds of things. Just don't yield to it. Cry out to Jesus for help! Just because the flesh gives you bad ideas or prompts you to have a nasty attitude, you do not have to give in. Our hearts are desperately wicked (Jer. 17:9). Satan is always going to try to cause you to sin with your thoughts and actions. You do not have to give in to it. Through Christ's power you can defeat him, so do not be frustrated. At first, when I became sensitive about loving without limits, it frustrated me. That is why I am giving you a warning, so you do not lose hope. I thought, "Wow, Lord, there's a lot of flesh here." He makes you sensitive to it so you can confess and repent of it and then walk in his love and power.

Now let me share an example in regards to a friend. I have a friend I am very close with—I love her, and she loves me. Well, sometimes situations arise where you hurt each other. When that happens, you have to decide whether you are going to continue your friendship or whether you are going to give it up. I was really wrestling with this because I felt (self again) that I was taken advantage of. She too had thoughts about me, which were not true. We could have gone our separate ways. However, God gave both of us the grace to put self aside. We both decided that although we really hurt each other, we needed to work things out and regain our friendship. We had to humble ourselves and take some steps to repair the damage. One thing I have found to be true is that when you decide to operate in God's agápe love, you will know it is none of you. Self is going to be put to death. You are going to be humbled over and over again. You get to a point where you say to yourself, "Okay, here we go." So you just go and do what God is prompting you to do, and you end up seeing Him move in mighty ways. Really! Although it may be hard at first, you find such peace and freedom in doing things God's ways. It does not make sense. I am at the point now where I may think, "I am going to look like a fool again." And I just go do it. You will find that when you do so, you will walk in such freedom, because you are not operating out of self.

I am happy this friend and I are continuously working to get back to where we used to be. You may have to do that. You may want all the sunshine in your life and not the rain. However, the rain and the suffering help you to really know God's love. If it was sunny all the time and everything went your way, you would not know how to *receive* and *give* God's love. You would not experience how He can keep you, how He is your refuge, or how He is your sustainer and your help. How would you know unless you needed Him in some way? We will experience suffering to some degree. Men's hearts are evil all the time, but God can use it to work His good (Rom. 8:28).

If you really love someone, you are not controlling them. That's not love. God loves you, and He does not control you (although in His sovereignty He can make everything work according to His plan). He allows you to have free choice, even to the point of your eternal destiny in accepting or rejecting His Son. So, it is up to you every moment of the day to make a choice of living for self or for your Savior. You have a choice to say, "Not this time, self."

God has given you the capacity to walk in this love, and this is what will bring blessings to you and your relationships. You will be victorious instead of defeated. When you get into the Word of God and study it, you will see encouragement about how at times you may be cast down, but you will not be forsaken (2 Cor. 4:9). You will see how a righteous man (women are not excluded) will fall seven times, but the Lord will pick him up (Prov. 24:16). You will become more confident and find this to be true if you will love without limits and not be governed by your feelings but by faith.

Faith Versus Feelings

Liz was petrified when her daughter Peggy concluded her announcement that Rosalyn was not only her roommate but her lover. A volcano of emotions erupted in the room, until Peggy grabbed Rosalyn's hand, and both stormed out the door. Liz collapsed on her husband's chest and wept. In just two years of college Peggy's morals had drastically diminished from those taught in her Christian home and youth group. What was Liz's relationship going to be now with Peggy? She had responded to Peggy out of her emotions and not at all in faith. She knew this situation with Peggy was known by God, and He alone would be able to rescue her from this lifestyle. Liz recognized her blocking a chance to reach Peggy and sought the Lord concerning what she should do next to restore connection with her daughter.

There are many situations that unfold in life whereby you may wish you had responded in faith and not your feelings. Relationships vertically and horizontally are affected by your responses of faith and feelings. As a matter of fact, faith operates in conjunction with love (1 Thes. 5:8 and 1 Tim. 1:14). God is a redeemer and is able to provide the grace needed in any situation where responding incorrectly with feelings has become detrimental. Yet, you should never take His grace for granted. There is much that can be said about not reacting out of your feelings but learning to respond in faith. The following is a short synopsis of a more detailed lesson available at our website on Faith vs. Feelings. I would recommend you go through this material, which has more details than could be shared here in the book. However, what is presented here should help you to begin to understand how important this area is in allowing your love light to shine.

It is important to state that emotions and feelings are not wrong, for they are created by God. Although God is Spirit and not a man, the Bible

Dropped but Not Broken

at times refers to Him in terms of having emotions. Psalm 147:11 says the Lord *delights* in those who fear Him. Ephesians 4:30 tells us not to *grieve* the Holy Spirit. So feelings and emotions are not wrong in and of themselves. It is when they are in control or dominate your life that sin occurs. What would the birth of a baby, a wedding, or any celebration be without the ability to express your feelings and emotions? Again, the problem comes when you allow them to override God. This happens when what you think, desire, will, or say takes precedence over what God thinks, desires, wills, or says.

There is a clear distinction between faith and feelings. Here are some things to be mindful of:

Feelings:

- Emanate from your soul (that part where the mind, will, and emotions reside).
- Can be negative or positive. For example:
    a. Positive—Can motivate you and help you to achieve or reach out to others.
    b. Negative—Can have you easily offended or cause you to withdraw from others.
    c. Can have you screaming, laughing, pouting, or sighing.
- Are spontaneous and can spring up with no conscious effort on your part at all. When they unexpectedly erupt, they can be very intense or subtle.
- Are unpredictable, deceitful, erratic, unstable, and changeable. They can be one way in the morning and different in the afternoon. They are unpredictable from one moment to the next.
- Are normally accompanied by physical changes such as: increased heartbeat, perspiration, headache, crying, depression, clenched teeth, raised blood pressure, etc.
- Should not be squashed or hidden, for they can cause you to implode internally and become ill.
- Are wonderful for revealing your soul's condition and weaknesses that need spiritual attention. When they become explosive, ask God to reveal to you why you responded in such a manner. The reason you exploded was because an

internal button was pushed. Find out what the button is and what God would have you to do to get the victory over this area in your life. This one step could heal a multitude of relationships.
- May appear real, but should never, never be the source of determining truth. God is the revealer of truth, not your feelings or intuition.
- Satan loves to work in the realm of your feelings—having you to rely on what you think, desire, will, or say over what God thinks, desires, wills, or says (John 10:10).

Faith:

- Is not intuition, positive thinking, impulses, gut feeling, a hunch, self-confidence, being optimistic, presumption, wishful thinking, or just stepping out blindly.
- The object of Biblical faith is God alone (Mark 11:22). Faith is having absolute confidence and trust in God. You believe He is who He says He is and that He will do what He says He will do. You believe you are what He says you are and you can do what He says you can do. It is having an intimate relationship with the living God of the universe (Eph. 2:8–10; Rom. 1:17). You do not have to have the absence of fear to exercise faith. You can feel fear and still step out in faith by trusting God in spite of the circumstances. Faith is not believing God can; it is knowing He will.
- It is a fruit of the Spirit (Gal. 5:22) and sword of the Spirit, which is the Word of God (Eph. 6:17). You cannot produce faith. The Spirit of God produces faith in you. You must cooperate with Him by submitting and yielding to His promptings in obedience.
- It is acting on the Word of God no matter how you feel. Faith does not operate apart from the Word. You must have a revelation from the Word to step out in faith. *"So then faith cometh by hearing, and hearing by the Word of God"* (Rom. 10:17, KJV). Faith is believing in what God says and does, and this is revealed in His Word and verified by His Spirit. God can do whatever He wants to do. He does speak in various ways, but those ways will *never* contradict what He

says in His Word. So the Word is an anchor when faith is in operation. Faith is always in conjunction with the Word of God. It is not stepping out blindly but stepping out on what God has revealed to you through His Word.
- It is the only way to please God (Heb. 11:6).
- Jesus is the author and finisher of your faith (Heb. 12:2). He was the initiator of it, and He will be the one to complete the work of faith in your life.
- It functions in two ways (Heb. 11:1):
    a. Concerning the future: *"substance of things hoped for."*
       It gives a sure foundation for what has not taken place yet (example: return of Jesus).
       You can stand firm on what you hope for—being sure of what you hope for.
    b. Concerning the present: *"evidence of things not seen."*
       It confirms and brings conviction of what you do not see presently (example: Jesus interceding on your behalf in Heaven).
       It is a present reality, even though you do not see it with your eyes—being certain of what you do not see presently.
- All Christians are given a measure of faith, even if it is the size of a mustard seed. Use what you have, and then you will grow. It is like a muscle. The more you exercise it, the stronger it gets. Jesus is faithful to provide the measure of faith you need for each task; you must trust Him and step out. Never compare your measure of faith to another. Each one has what is necessary for their call and God's plan. Keep your eyes on Him!
- It is knowing that no matter what happens, God will never leave you or forsake you. It means accepting everything that happens to you as allowed by God, knowing He will use it for your good and His glory.
- Satan desires to destroy our faith in God, for your entire Christian walk is based on faith (2 Cor. 5:7). Faith is the means by which we overcome. *"For whatsoever is born of God*

overcometh the world: and this is the victory that overcometh the world, even our faith" (1 John 5:4, KJV).

The world says, "Seeing is believing." God basically lets us know, "Believing is seeing." You may want to understand and then believe, but you must believe and then the understanding will come. Jesus said to Martha, *"Did I not tell you that if you believed, you would see the glory of God?"* (John 11:40, NIV). In spiritual matters faith precedes understanding.

The purpose of Transformed Worldwide Ministries (the teaching ministry I am a director of) is to provide practical teaching material on the Word of God (see www.twmforjesus.org). The following material is an example of how we try to break doctrine down into an easy format to remember so you can live it out each day. Faith and feelings will be broken down into three steps so you can remember and be sensitive to them when situations arise in your life.

The following diagrams will show what takes place when you *naturally* respond to situations and are governed by your **feelings**.

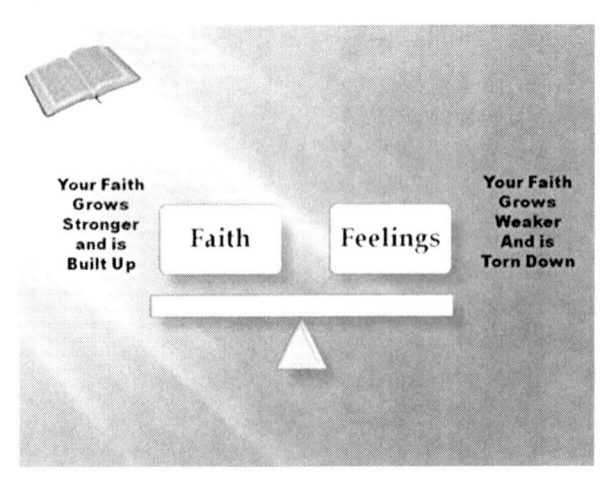

An unexpected situation arises in your life. You have a choice to react with your feelings or respond in faith. If you respond in faith, your faith grows stronger, and you are built up. If you react with your feelings, your faith grows weaker, and you become torn down. The Bible in the upper left corner represents the Word of God shining down on your faith and feelings. All of life's decisions are based on accepting or rejecting what God says in His Word. Faith and feelings are placed on a scale to illustrate that one or the other will weigh heavily in your decision making. When faith is strong, the scale will tip to the left, and when feelings are strong, the scale will tip to the right. This is just for illustration purposes. If you were asked, "Which side weighs heavier in your life right now?" What would you say? Do you allow what you think, desire, will, or say to take precedence over what God thinks, desires, wills, or says?

Hebrews 4:12 (NIV) states, *"For the word of God is living and active. Sharper than any double-edged sword, it penetrates even to dividing soul and spirit."* It takes the Word of God to help you to divide or distinguish between what is of your soul and what is of your spirit. Feelings emanate from your soul, and faith emanates from your spirit. Only God's living Word will help you to know when you are operating out of your feelings or out of your faith. Your spirit is in reference to the Spirit of God, which should be controlling your life through faith. This is why a Christian cannot live a holy life apart from God's Word.

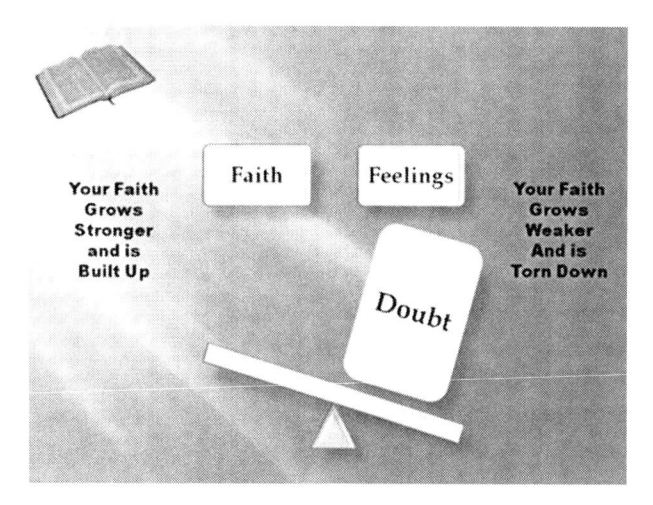

Step #1:

You react with your feelings. The scale tips to the right. Doubt has taken place. Doubt means you have a double mind or are caught between two opinions—God's opinion and your own opinion. "I know

God wants me to … , but I want to …" Somehow you doubt what He says or what he says He will do. Deliberately or unconsciously you have not accepted or trusted what God has said over what you are feeling. You have not taken the way of escape provided by Him (1 Cor. 10:13). *"But let him ask in faith, nothing wavering. For he that wavereth is like a wave of the sea driven with the wind and tossed. For let not that man think that he shall receive any thing of the Lord. A double minded man is unstable in all his ways"* (James 1:6–8, KJV). Notice that when you are oscillating between what God has said and what you are feeling, you have become unstable and will not receive anything of the Lord. This going back and forth between the two is revealing doubt in your heart. A Christian woman may say, "I know he is doing drugs, but he is so cute, and I can help him."

The person who has not initially trusted Jesus for salvation will not trust Him for the other things in his or her life either. The Word of God is foolishness to him/her because they cannot understand it without God's Spirit dwelling within them. They would have no choice but to operate out of their feelings. Living by feelings does not have to be taught to a person, he or she will do it naturally. *"But the natural man receiveth not the things of the Spirit of God: for they are foolishness unto him: neither can he know them, because they are spiritually discerned"* (1 Cor. 2:14, KJV).

When any of the Word is not received with faith, it will not benefit you. *"For we also have had the gospel preached to us, just as they did; but the message they heard was of no value to them, because those who heard did not combine it with faith"* (Heb. 4:2, NIV). When you doubt you are not having absolute confidence and trust in God; you have entered into sin. *"For whatsoever is not of faith is sin"* (Rom. 14:23, KJV). Whenever you do anything without faith in God, you are on the wrong path. There are times when you may not be confidently sure if you are doing exactly what God wants you to do, even after you have asked for wisdom and sought His guidance. At those times, you should both be still and wait, or if you are in a situation where you must take action immediately you step out with what knowledge you do have from the Lord and trust Him to protect and guide. Only He knows your heart and true motivation. If you are sincere in seeking His will and get off the path, He will lovingly instruct and correct you to get back on the right path. This is what His mercy and grace are all about. Do not picture Him with a sledgehammer

Dropped but Not Broken

ready to pound you to the ground, but picture Him with an outstretched hand ready to help restore you.

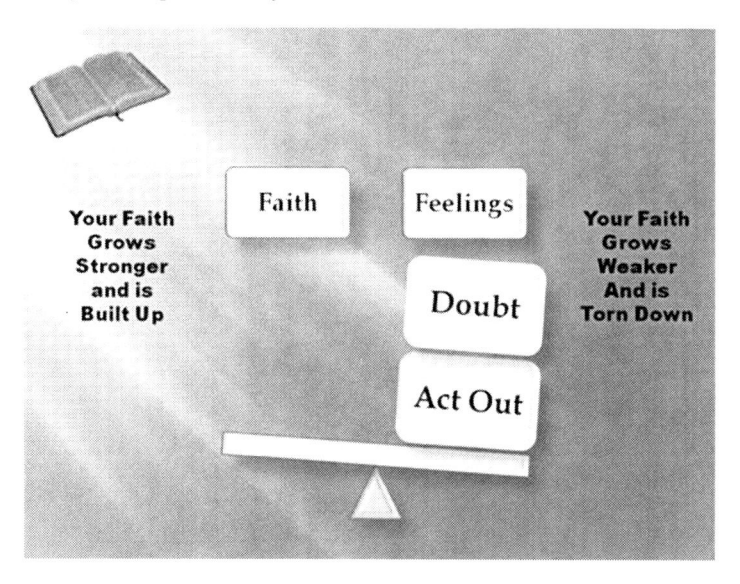

[Illustration: A balance scale with "Faith" and "Feelings", "Doubt", "Act Out" blocks. Left side: "Your Faith Grows Stronger and is Built Up". Right side: "Your Faith Grows Weaker And is Torn Down".]

Step #2:

Once doubt has taken place in your mind, it will be seen in your actions. *"For as he thinks in his heart, so is he"* (Prov. 23:7, NKJV). This proverb lets us know that what you think, you become. What you believe in your heart will be revealed in your speech, actions, and attitude. Your thoughts shape your life. If you do not believe or trust what God has said, and you lean on your own understanding, you will reap the consequences of that choice.

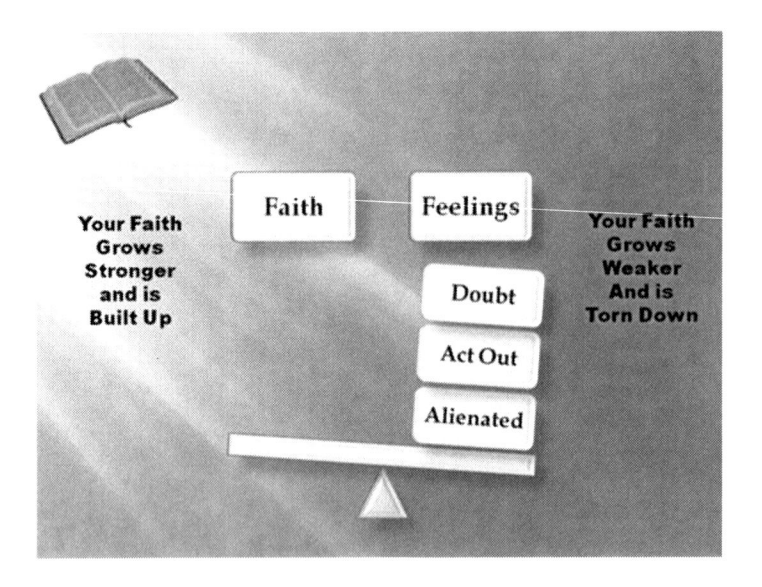

Step #3:

When doubt overrides faith in God, your actions and behavior will follow, and then, as a result of your disobedience, you will become alienated from God. Your fellowship with Him will be broken. You will not function in the full anointing of His Spirit. You will see an absence of His power in your life and may even blame Him for it. You may not sense His love, but it is you who has moved away from Him. He remains the same and is waiting for you to turn back to Him. When you draw back to Him, He will draw back to you (James 4:8). The pleasure of sin is for a season, but God's way is best and is everlasting. The longer you remain in this state, the weaker your faith will become.

Dropped but Not Broken

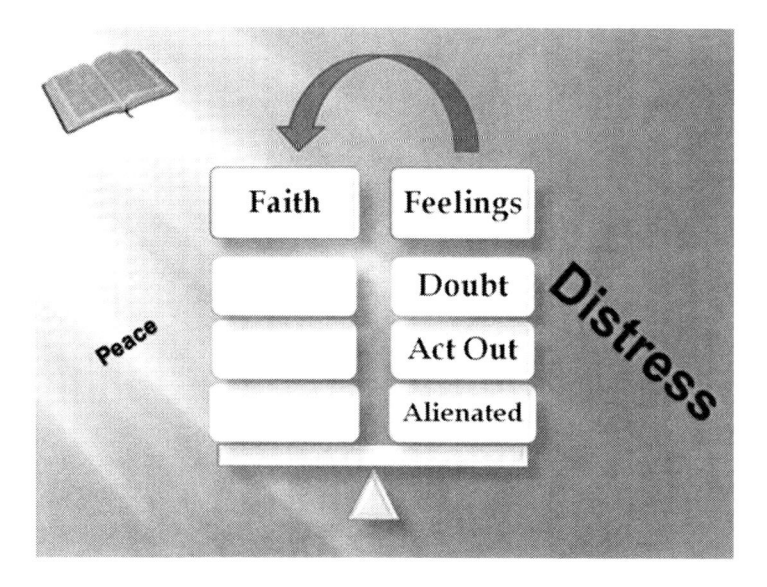

[Diagram: A balance scale tipped to the right. Left side (raised) labeled "Faith" with "Peace" written along the tilted beam. Right side (lowered) labeled "Feelings," "Doubt," "Act Out," "Alienated" with "Distress" written along the tilted beam. An open Bible sits above with a curved arrow pointing down toward the "Feelings" side.]

This picture illustrates feelings overriding your faith (see arrow) and what results when this happens. When your feelings dominate over your faith, that will lead to distress and lack of peace in your life. You may even feel you are justified in not trusting Him should your circumstances turn for the worse. When feelings dominate your faith, you will *feel* disappointed with Jesus. Although these are not true, here are some ways you may feel disappointed in Him:

- You feel He was too late and not there when you needed Him.
- You cannot understand the death of your loved one.
- He did not protect you in the way you thought.
- You feel He dashed your dreams or plans.
- You wonder if He really cares.
- You feel He has left you.
- You feel He is not what you thought He would be.
- You feel He requires too much.

Now in contrast, the following diagrams will show what takes place when you *supernaturally* respond to situations and are governed by your **faith**:

Paula Harris

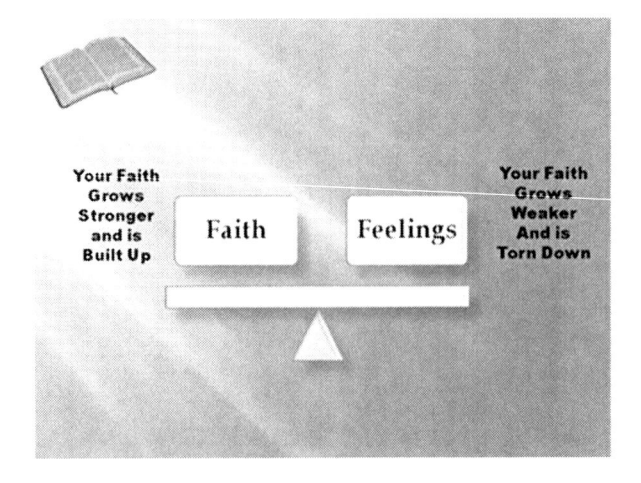

[Illustration: A balance scale with "Faith" and "Feelings" blocks level. Left label: "Your Faith Grows Stronger and is Built Up". Right label: "Your Faith Grows Weaker And is Torn Down".]

An unexpected situation arises in your life. You have a choice to react with your feelings or respond in faith. If you respond in faith, your faith grows stronger, and you are built up. If you react with your feelings, your faith grows weaker and you become torn down.

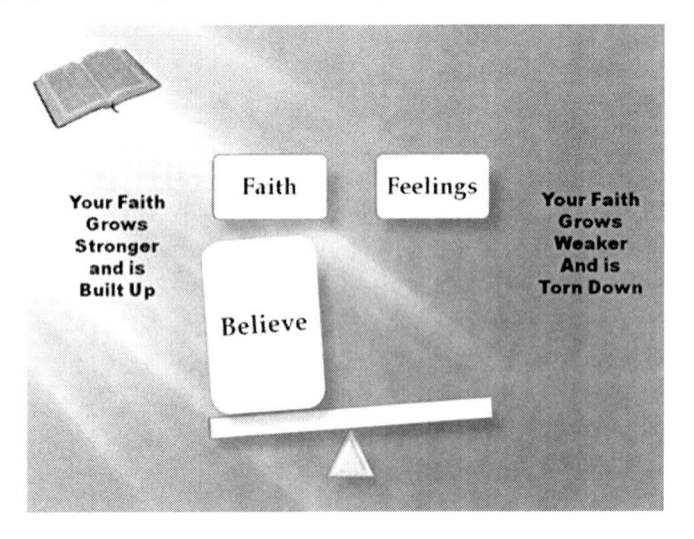

[Illustration: A balance scale tipped to the left with a large "Believe" block on the Faith side. Left label: "Your Faith Grows Stronger and is Built Up". Right label: "Your Faith Grows Weaker And is Torn Down".]

Step #1:

You respond in faith. The scale tips to the left. You believe and confidently trust God is who He says He is and will do what He says He will do. You honor His Word above your feelings. You exercise the amount of faith that you have at the present. *"For I say, through the grace given to me, to everyone who is among you, not to think of himself more*

Dropped but Not Broken

highly than he ought to think, but to think soberly, as God has dealt to each one a measure of faith" (Rom. 12:3, NKJV). You will be able to say as the Apostle Paul that you "**know**," you "**believe**," you are "**persuaded**," and are convinced that "**He is able**" regardless of how bad the situation may look. *"For this reason I also suffer these things; nevertheless I am not ashamed, for I know whom I have believed and am persuaded that He is able to keep what I have committed to Him until that Day"* (2 Tim. 1:12, NKJV). Just like Abraham you did not waiver in your faith. *"He did not waver at the promise of God through unbelief, but was strengthened in faith, giving glory to God"* (Rom. 4:20, NKJV). You did not waver between what God said versus what you were feeling. Your faith grows, and others grow as they watch your walk of faith, just as your faith is strengthened when you observe the faith of others.

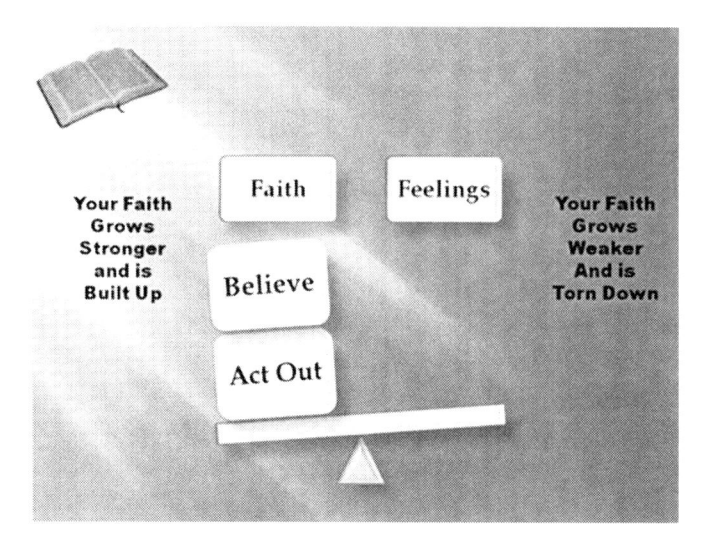

Step #2:

Once faith has taken place in your mind, it will be seen in your actions. *"What good is it, dear brothers and sisters, if you say you have faith but don't show it by your actions? Can that kind of faith save anyone? Suppose you see a brother or sister who has no food or clothing, and you say, 'Good-bye and have a good day; stay warm and eat well'—but then you don't give that person any food or clothing. What good does that do? So you see, faith by itself isn't enough. Unless it produces good deeds, it is dead and useless"* (James 2:14–17, NLT). *"We having the same spirit of faith, according as it is written, I believed, and therefore have I spoken; we also believe, and therefore speak"*

(2 Cor. 4:13, KJV). What you believe in your heart, will be revealed in your speech, actions, and attitude. If you believe and trust what God has said, and you do not lean on your own understanding, you will reap the rewards of your choice.

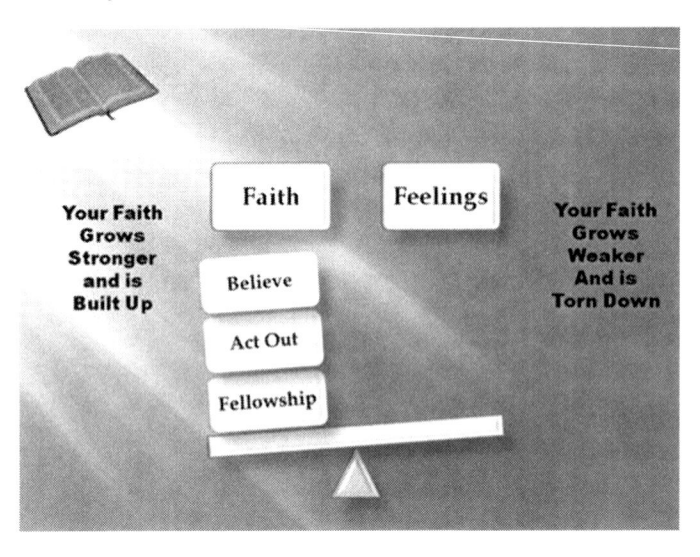

Step #3:

When faith in God overrides your feelings, your actions and behavior will follow, and then as a result of your obedience you will remain in fellowship with God. Your fellowship with Him will not be broken. You will function in the full anointing of His Spirit. *"So you must remain faithful to what you have been taught from the beginning. If you do, you will remain in fellowship with the Son and with the Father. And in this fellowship we enjoy the eternal life he promised us"* (1 John 2:24–25, NLT). Your intimacy with Him will not be interrupted as you commune with Him throughout the day, seeing Him ordering your steps, making a way out of no way, and helping you to overcome the evil that arises against you. You will both delight in each other.

Dropped but Not Broken

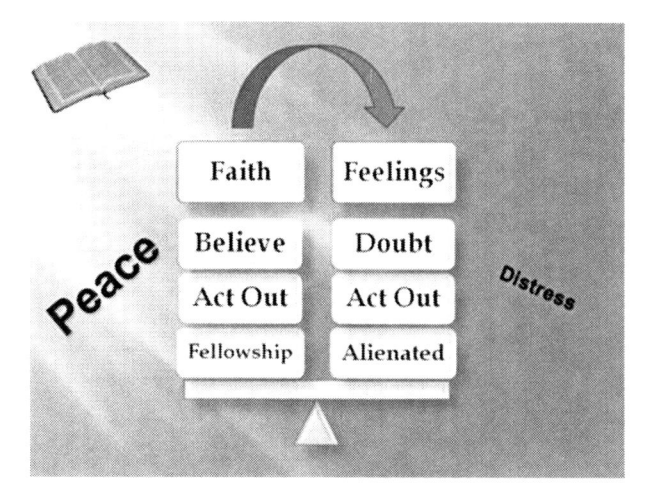

[Diagram: A balance scale with an open Bible above it. An arrow curves from "Faith" side to "Feelings" side. Left side stack (labeled "Peace"): Faith / Believe / Act Out / Fellowship. Right side stack (labeled "Distress"): Feelings / Doubt / Act Out / Alienated.]

This picture illustrates faith overriding your feelings (see arrow) and what results when this happens. When your faith dominates over your feelings, it will then lead to peace and lack of distress in your life. Should your outward circumstances turn for the worse, you will still have an inner peace that is unexplainable by man (Phil. 4:7). Your life is so much better when you live this way. When faith dominates your feelings, you will *believe* what Jesus has said and done regardless of the consequences in your life. Here are some ways you may feel encouraged in Him:

- You believe He is never late.
- You accept though you do not understand the death of your loved one.
- You understand His ways are not your ways, and His thoughts are not your thoughts.
- You know if your dreams or plans are dashed, He is protecting you or providing a better way.
- You know and trust his care for you even when you cannot see it clearly.
- You are confident He has not left you.
- You are assured, though He is different from what you first thought, He is faithful.
- You are thankful that what He requires, He has already provided.

The more you trust and believe in His Word, the less you will be governed by your feelings. This is supernatural indeed and, again, cannot be done just because you determine to do so in your own strength. You will naturally take the three steps of responding by your feelings, or you will supernaturally take the three steps of responding by faith. Ask the Lord to make you more sensitive to what three steps you are taking throughout the day. Detect when you are allowing your feelings to take control. Your love light will shine when you are walking by faith and not your feelings.

Faith Overcoming Feelings

Faith — Believe — Act Out — Fellowship

Feelings — Doubt — Act Out — Alienated

GOD'S AMAZING GRACE!

I have a cloth banner hanging in my home that says, "God is faithful to all of His promises." It would be good for you to ask yourself at this moment, "Is He faithful to all of His promises?" That question needs to be settled once and for all in your heart. When it is, you will be able to trust Him no matter what comes into your life.

I highly recommend that you go to our website to listen to this lesson in its entirety. It will bring a blessing to your soul. You are not being asked to crucify all of your emotions but to not let them dominate or overrule God's will for your life. Another lesson, entitled "Who Touched My Clothes," is available through our ministry to strengthen your faith as well. When you learn to live this way, your relationships will thrive as well. Many relationships have suffered by one or both parties bombarding the other with a slingshot of emotions. Faith will help you keep your sanity regardless of others' tantrums. This is important, for faith is the beginning and ending of your entire Christian walk. Luke 18:8 (KJV) states, *"I tell you that he will avenge them speedily. Nevertheless when the Son of man cometh, shall he find faith on the earth?"* When Jesus returns, will He find faith on the earth? Will you be the one to say, "I do" in wanting your faith to shine forth on this earth for Jesus?

"I Do"

Katherine stretched out her arms and her toes as she lay in bed with the sun glimmering on the aqua tones of her bedspread. This was it. This was the day she would say "I do" to Tom. She reminisced about what led up to this day of committing the rest of her life to one man. What a big commitment! A mixture of fear and tranquility sweep over her. Although the unknown spurred the fear, it would subside when she reflected upon Tom's commitment to her and his resilience to never leave her unprotected. The commitment was big on both their parts but was one worth making.

As a result of God's love being rejected and distorted by many in this present age, much time has been spent in this book defining what agápe love is and how to recognize it. It has been explained that it is real and available to you for all eternity. You cannot work to obtain or maintain it; it is a free gift.

It is not by chance you are reading this book. God knew you would. At this moment picture Him stretching His arms out to you with compassionate love on His face. He bends down to your level and asks, "Will you commit to a lifelong love relationship with Me? (After all, you are My bride.) Will you say, "I do" or "I don't think so?" When a bride says "I do" to the groom, she has agreed to enter into a covenant for life.

Do you understand the lifelong commitment God has made with you? Hebrews 8:10–12 (NLT) states, *"But this is the new covenant I will make with the people of Israel on that day, says the* Lord*: I will put my laws in their minds, and I will write them on their hearts. I will be their God, and they will be my people. And they will not need to teach their neighbors, nor will they need to teach their relatives, saying, 'You should know the* Lord*.'*

For everyone, from the least to the greatest, will know me already. And I will forgive their wickedness, and I will never again remember their sins." He will never again remember your sins! That which blocked your love relationship with Him has been dealt with forever! He took the initiative and did everything that was necessary to restore you to Himself for all eternity!

Hebrews 10:11–14 (KJV) says, *"And every priest standeth daily ministering and offering oftentimes the same sacrifices, which can never take away sins; But this man, after he had offered one sacrifice for sins forever, sat down on the right hand of God. From henceforth expecting till his enemies be made his footstool. For by one offering he hath perfected forever them that are sanctified."* Now look at the same passage in another translation.

Hebrews 10:11–14 (NLT) says, *"Under the Old Covenant, the priest stands and ministers before the altar day after day, offering the same sacrifices again and again, which can never take away sins. But our High Priest offered himself to God as a single sacrifice for sins, good for all time. Then he sat down in the place of honor at God's right hand. There he waits until his enemies are humbled and made a footstool under his feet. For by that one offering he forever made perfect those who are being made holy."*

You can see your High Priest, Jesus Christ, is different from the Old Testament high priests. He offered Himself to God **once** as a sacrifice for our sins. That **one** sacrifice does not need to be repeated, but is good for all time (eternity). When it says He has sat down, that is symbolic of His work being completed. Since there is no more work needed to deal with our sins (for He satisfied **all** of God's holy requirements for punishing sin in mankind), He is seated at the right hand of God. The right hand is symbolic of the place of honor and respect. God has honored the Son by allowing Him this position. Jesus has satisfied, **once for all**, God's holy wrath against sin. He took your place and paid your sin debt by taking the punishment that was due you and placed it upon Himself so you could go free. One day all of His enemies (Satan and his host of demons) will be put under His feet. Until then, His finished work on the cross (that one offering) has made all who believe in His sacrifice on their behalf declared "perfect" before God. Second Corinthians 5:21 (NIV), states, *"God made Him (Jesus) who had no sin to be sin for us, so in Him we might become the righteousness of God."*

Now look at Hebrews 10:14 (NLT) again, "For by that one offering he forever made perfect those who are being made holy." It seems contradictory to say Christians **are forever made perfect** and then say they **are being made holy.** Either they are, or they are not. The "are forever made perfect" means Christians are forever declared perfect in God's sight. They can approach and have communion with a Holy God because judgment for their sins has been settled, and they are now declared holy by the sacrificial death of Jesus Christ. Therefore, *positionally* Christians are in right *relationship* with God and not under His wrath anymore. However, *practically*, they still commit acts of sin that hinder *fellowship* with God. That is what is meant by "are being made holy." Although in position they are in right relationship with God (it is final), the practical everyday fellowship with God is still being worked out (it is progressive). God's Holy Spirit is transforming their lives continuously until one day they match completely what they have been declared by God—holy and without blame before Him in love (Eph. 1:4). This is normally referred to as the sanctification process of a Christian, while the positional part is referred to as salvation. The progression is salvation, sanctification, and then glorification. Glorification is when they will have a glorified body, be delivered from sin completely, and see Jesus face to face in His glory.

Here is an illustration to help you understand this passage. When a healthy baby is born, she has all of her body parts. She is whole. However, she is going to have many opportunities to develop and use each body part. In Christ, you are born again and made whole in Him. However, you will have many opportunities while still on earth to develop and use each spiritual body part. A baby does not come out of the womb and start sprinting down the street, and neither will you do so spiritually. It will take time to crawl, walk, and then sprint in the Spirit and overcome your fleshly desires.

So this is the lifelong commitment God has made to you. He has saved you and is sanctifying you until the day when He will glorify you. He has in the past loved you, is now loving you, and will always love you. The bridegroom (Mark 2:19) has said to you, "I do." He has been and is fully committed to you.

The question again is will you be fully committed to Him? Have you said, "I do?" Do you love the Lord your God with all your heart and

Dropped but Not Broken

with all your soul and with all your mind? How do you begin to do this? Jesus gives you the answer in John, chapters 14 and 15 (NKJV), (some passages noted below):

> *If you love Me, keep My commandments. He who has My commandments and keeps them, it is he who loves Me. Jesus answered and said to him, "If anyone loves Me, he will keep My word. He who does not love Me does not keep My words." As the Father loved Me, I also have loved you; abide in My love. If you keep My commandments, you will abide in My love, just as I have kept My Father's commandments and abide in His love.*

I so appreciate how our Lord does not complicate things. Do you want to show your love for Him? Then keep His commandments. If you do not keep His commandments, then it says you do not really love Him. Plain and simple. In the section "Yes, You Can" you saw how He even works in you to accomplish this. So He gives you commandments and then works in you to fulfill them. Your part is to obey and cooperate with Him every time He prompts you by His Spirit to do something. If you will learn to swiftly obey each time He commands you to do something, then you will be expressing your love for Him. When you know He is prompting or commanding you to do something, and you refuse to obey, then you are expressing a lack of love for Him.

Your obedience is not done to gain acceptance by God; your obedience is an expression of your love for Him. Do you see how this is different from performing to gain brownie points with God? Out of love Christ has completed all the work necessary on your part; now your obedience is an expression of your love back to Him. It is also a statement of your acceptance and confidence in the work He has completed on your behalf. So you cease from striving to perform to gain acceptance or approval, and your energy is now put into obeying Him as an expression of your love. Galatians 3:3 (NLT) says, *"How foolish can you be? After starting your Christian lives in the Spirit, why are you now trying to become perfect by your own human effort?"* So His love motivates your obedience, and your obedience expresses your love.

There is so much that can be said about obedience and the power of God's Holy Spirit working in you. Yet, Jesus has once again simplified things for us by taking all of the commandments and condensing them into two main commandments that we must keep. Here they are again:

Matthew 22:37–40 (NIV), *"Jesus replied: 'Love the Lord your God with all your heart and with all your soul and with all your mind.' This is the first and greatest commandment. And the second is like it: 'Love your neighbor as yourself.' All the Law and the Prophets hang on these two commandments."* Do you see that? All that has been taught by the law and the prophets is condensed into these two commandments: (1) you are to love God, and (2) you are to love others as yourself. That is it! The entire Bible teaches how to obey these two commandments. So these two commandments should be your focal point continuously. This whole book has been written to help you focus on obeying these two commandments and to give you the practical image of the cross to remember them. It was written to give you wisdom on how to have a love relationship with God (vertical) which will in turn bless your relationships with others (horizontal). Once again, focusing on the horizontal relationships without the vertical upholding them will lead to disaster. The other relationships will not be sustained. They cannot fully satisfy you apart from you having a relationship with God. Have you said "I do?" Will you commit to obeying these commandments and express your love back to Him?

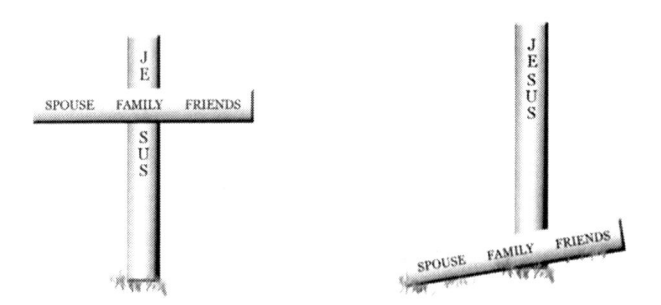

Maybe you are saying, "I said 'I do' a long time ago, but I keep sinning. I know He is frustrated with me, because I continuously fail in my obedience. My relationship with Him and others is not what it should be. I do love Him in my heart, but my actions are not expressing my love for Him, and I am failing to love others too. I feel so guilty and shameful of my behavior. I am trying so hard." Take a breath, relax, and listen. God knows all about your failures. That is why Jesus took care of your past, present, and future sins. He took care of them for eternity. Now that does not give you the freedom to just go and continue in sin (Rom. 6:1). If you really love the Lord, you will obey His commandments. You will not want to live a life of sin. There is a difference between sporadic acts of sin and just having a lifestyle of sinfulness. However, when you do sin, His Word instructs what you should do. First John 1:9 (NKJV) states, *"If we confess our sins, He is faithful and just to forgive us our sins and to cleanse us from all unrighteousness."* When you sin now as a Christian, it does not take away your relationship with God (salvation), but it does affect your present fellowship with God (sanctification). Remember Hebrews 10:14 (NLT), *"For by that one offering he forever made perfect those who are being made holy."* You will not be perfectly free from sinning until you meet the Lord in glory. Right now, like the baby we discussed, you are learning to crawl, walk, and run spiritually. When a toddler makes a mistake and falls and breaks something, the parent does not punish the baby and say, "Okay, you are finished! Don't you ever try to walk again!" A loving parent will pick the baby up and correct it by teaching it how to walk so the baby does not get hurt and so the baby does not break anything. Likewise, if a daughter disobeys her mother, that does not end her relationship as a daughter in the family. However, it will cause a break in fellowship until the daughter comes back to the mother and gets things right with her.

God is a faithful parent. When you come and acknowledge the wrong you have done (confess your sins), He will be faithful every time to forgive your sins and cleanse you from all unrighteousness by applying the finished work of Jesus on the cross to your disobedience. Then He will remember your sin no more. He has promised this over and over in the Bible. You just have to believe it and go and purpose not to continuously live in sin.

First John 1:5–10 gives us further wisdom in this area. It says God is light, and there is no darkness in Him at all. This light represents righteousness and His holy domain. A person cannot say they are a Christian and live continuously in the darkness of sin (representing unrighteous and Satan's domain). Verse 6 says such a person is a liar and is not walking according to truth. She is deceived into thinking she can belong to both domains at the same time. Christians have been removed from darkness and placed into the Holy light of God. That is how they are able to have fellowship with Him. Now when a Christian sins, that person has stepped back *temporarily* into the realm of darkness, where they do not belong. Yet because of Jesus, that person is able to agree with God that what they did was wrong (confess their sin) and be restored back into the light with God. If a person *dwells* in darkness, they are not a Christian. A Christian who has been removed from darkness is not comfortable in the darkness. They will be miserable until they come back to where they belong. John 5:24 (NLT) confirms, *"I tell you the truth, those who listen to my message and believe in God who sent me have eternal life. They will never be condemned for their sins, but they have already passed from death into life."* You are not condemned when you commit acts of sin after salvation. Your salvation cannot be taken away from you (Rom. 8:30). However, you will harm your fellowship with God when you sin. Confess sin immediately, knowing the forgiveness Jesus purchased for you on the cross is applied. First Peter 2:24–25 (NLT) says, *"He personally carried our sins in his body on the cross so that we can be dead to sin and live for what is right. By his wounds you are healed. Once you were like sheep who wandered away. But now you have turned to your Shepherd, the Guardian of your souls."*

I would like for you to prayerfully consider something in regard to confessing your sins. Now that you are a Christian, what are you thinking about when you ask God to *forgive* you of your sins? Doctrinally, to be a Christian, you would have had your sins totally forgiven and removed by the shed blood of Jesus Christ. For without the shedding of blood, there is no remission (forgiveness) of sins. Hebrews 10:18 (KJV) says, *"Now where remission of these is, there is no more offering for sin."* The sin matter is settled and no more offerings are necessary. In the earlier passages read, you saw that by the one sacrifice of Jesus, He removed your sins *forever*. He, unlike the other priests, does not have to offer a sacrifice continuously. Then why is it any Christian would pray in a manner that appears to have Jesus forgive their sins *each time* they commit them after salvation? Did He not take care of all their sins past, present, and future with one sacrifice? Did He not declare them perfect and righteous before God? Need He repeatedly deal with their sin even after they become a Christian? Was it or was it not settled on the cross at Calvary? Since blood was shed on the Day of Atonement once a year for forgiveness of sins (Lev. 16:33–34), cannot the blood of Jesus, the Son of God, cleanse sins for all eternity and not just from one sin to the next? The Word of God says His one sacrifice perfected them forever (Heb. 10:11–14)!

Does 1 John tell us to *ask for forgiveness* of sin? No, it tells us to *confess* our sins. To confess means to acknowledge and agree with God that what we did wrong was sin. It means to say the same thing about our sin as He would say. Here we go again. It seems we are straining at a gnat, but these doctrinal things are important. The more you get to know Jesus through His Word, the less you want to offend Him in any area of your life. I personally feel many Christians may not know how offensive it is to say you acknowledge the redemptive work of Jesus on the cross but daily act as if He is *at that very moment* forgiving each sin as each sin is mentioned. To me it is almost as if they are crucifying Him afresh—over and over again with each confessed sin. Did He handle your sin debt at the cross or not? Is it finished? Then why continue a mind-set of sins being forgiven on a daily or moment-by-moment basis?

There are several Greek words in regards to forgiveness. A few are: (1) *charizomai*, meaning "to forgive sins"; *aphesis*, meaning "putting it away" (denotes the discharge of a debt—sin is considered a debt); and *paresis*, meaning "passing over" (God not executing full retribution called for by sin but instead showing mercy). You may say, "All right already, why do we have to get into all of this?" In any love relationship you guard your words so as not to offend the other person. Have you ever thought in your conversation with Jesus you may say something that is offensive to Him—something that mocks the very expression of His love for you? Now our Lord is not petty, but I cannot help but wonder about this issue. If I made provision for my child to go to college (all expenses paid), and my child kept expressing worry over what I had already provided, I would be hurt. The more you draw closer to Jesus and see the commitment of love He has for you and all that He has done on your behalf, you will not take it for granted. Neither will you want to hurt or grieve Him in any way. The more you come to understand His love, the more you want to love Him back. Just by chance, could

He be grieved over anyone constantly acting like He did not complete His work on the cross? Would it not sadden His heart?

Now that you are a Christian, what should you do when you sin? This passage gives insight: *"For godly sorrow worketh repentance to salvation not to be repented of: but the sorrow of the world worketh death"* (2 Cor. 7:10, KJV). You see, there is to be a godly sorrow over your sin. Jesus died so you would be released from the power of sin over your life. Your act of sin has grieved Him (Eph. 4:30) and it should grieve you. (The kind of sorrow that is not godly sorrow is the type of sorrow that comes from regret when you get caught in an act of sin. You have sorrow only because you got caught, not because you acted against God. That is not godly sorrow.)

Continuing with the Scripture, *"godly sorrow worketh repentance."* When you are truly sorry over grieving God, that kind of sorrow leads to your going in a different moral direction (repentance). You do not continue in your sin; you have a change of mind and heart by going in a new direction. So instead of continuing to turn away from God, you now turn back to God. You desire to have your fellowship restored with Him.

Continuing with the Scripture, *"that leads to salvation."* Not salvation of your soul from the condemnation of hell (you already have that). Salvation (being saved from) here describes deliverance from any type of sin, bondage, or affliction in a person's life.

Continuing with the Scripture, *"not to be repented of."* The words "repented of" here have a different meaning; they mean to have no regret. So when you are truly grieved over what you did to break your fellowship with God, you fully acknowledge your sin, calling it what He calls it; it leads to your having a change of mind and heart back to Him, and in the end you will not regret having done this.

Of course, this mind-set is expressed in prayer to God. This takes us all the way back to what I wanted you to consider in regards to how you express your repentance before Him. Remember 1 John 1:9 did not instruct us to "ask for forgiveness" but to "confess" our sins. It then states what God will do. He will be faithful (every time) and just (having already judged our sins on the cross) to forgive (continuously apply the forgiveness already secured by Jesus's shed blood for) our sins and cleanse us from all unrighteousness (to deliver us from anything that is not right with Him and hinders our fellowship). I am basically suggesting that you pay attention to your mind-set when praying regarding your sins. At the moment of confession, recognize you are being cleansed from anything that has hindered your fellowship with Him. First John 1:7 helps you understand you are only able to have fellowship with God and those in the family of God by continuously being cleansed by the shed blood of Jesus Christ. The phrase "cleanses us from all sin" is a continuous action.

Would I go so far as to say it is wrong to ask for forgiveness when praying? No. Luke 11:4 and Matthew 6:12 have petitions for forgiveness. The same Greek word for "forgive," *aphiēmi*, used in these two passages is also used in 1 John 1:9 when it states God is just to "forgive." It means to "let go; send away." A thorough study of these two passages with 1 John 1:9 will not reveal any conflict but an obvious difference.

The Christian in Luke 11:2–4 and Matthew 6:9–13, *is in worshipful fellowship* with her Father and praying her forgiveness (the letting go and sending away of her sins) be continuous as she continuously forgives (lets go and sends away) the sins against her. We know this person is already in fellowship by how this prayer begins. In addition, she asks in the following verse to be delivered from any temptation that would cause sin and broken fellowship. This Christian wants to *continue* to benefit from her sin having been sent away. Note further down in Matthew 6:14–15, she knows her fellowship with God *will be broken* if she refuses to extend forgiveness (let go of the sin of others) as well. Having already been forgiven by God, she has an obligation to forgive others. That is why you may see the words "forgive us our debts **as** we forgive" or "forgive us our sins **for** we also forgive," depending on the translation.

In contrast, the situation in 1 John 1:9 is a Christian who *already has broken fellowship* with God. That is why she needs to confess to be cleansed and restored.

As a Christian you may still chose to continue to use the words "forgive me" as you confess sin. I would like to ask: "Are your sins just forgiven when you ask? What if you overlook or are not aware of a specific sin in your heart? What if you die before asking for forgiveness of a sin? Can a Christian have some leftover sins that were not dealt with at Calvary? Can there be any future sin that could have escaped Jesus's sight? I do not claim to understand it all, but we need to seriously consider what is being expressed in our prayers. Hopefully, with what has been pointed out, your thoughts will not be that your forgiveness is dependent upon your moment-by-moment petition for forgiveness. Instead, you will confess as instructed because you have offended Jesus and are asking Him to cleanse your temporary collapse into sin so your fellowship may be restored. Let me give you an example of how this may change the way in which you pray. This is just an example to drive home a point.

When seeking forgiveness at the moment of prayer, you might pray: "Lord Jesus, *please forgive me for gossiping.* I am sorry for sinning against You. *Please forgive me now* for my sin and cleanse me *now.* I thank you for forgiving me and ask that you give me strength to not sin against You again."

Instead, knowing that your sins are forgiven but seeking your fellowship to be restored, you might pray: "Lord Jesus *I acknowledge my sin of gossiping.* I am sorry for grieving You. *I thank you for your forgiveness and for cleansing me from all my sin.* I ask that you strengthen me that I may not sin against You again."

Do you see the difference? In the second prayer you are already acknowledging what Jesus has done for you. You are honoring His work on the cross and expressing what He has said over and over again in His Word about your sins. When you step out of the light of His fellowship, you need to specifically and remorsefully acknowledge what you did. Call it what He calls it—sin. Then thank Him for the forgiveness *you already have* in Christ (believe what He has said in His Word). Then by faith set out to obey His commandments once again.

Let me sum this up, and you can look at the previous Scriptures in reference to what I am saying, and by all means pray and ask God to give you insight into what is being said. Jesus has taken care of all your sins on the cross by His resurrection forever. No more forgiveness of sin is needed when you by faith receive redemption through Christ. Although Christians have been forgiven of their sin debt once and for all time, they still commit acts of sin. When that happens, they need to acknowledge each act of sin immediately. Their sin debt was in relationship to salvation, the acts of sin after salvation have to do with sanctification and daily fellowship with God (1 Cor. 1:9).

This may not seem like anything to be concerned about. For you it may not be, but for others it has been a deep challenge. One day when I was in my quiet time and thinking of His commitment to redeem all of us who were lost, my heart overflowed with joy and praise for the wonderful work He *finished* on the cross. I do not want my way of thinking or words expressed to reveal anything less.

I trust at this point you have said, "I do" to Jesus. When you received Jesus as your Lord and Savior, that is really when you said "I do." It was then you entered into the New Covenant relationship we discussed earlier in the book. A covenant is not to be broken or disannulled like a contract. And even though the New Covenant is not based upon your works, does that mean you have no responsibility at all toward God? No, it does not mean that you are released of responsibility. Although the New Covenant is not based upon your performing deeds to be acceptable to God, you have a responsibility to obey the commandments of God on a daily basis. Your obeying His commands is an expression of your love for Him. It is the way you remain in the light of His fellowship.

Now if you decide to remain in the dark too long by not dealing with your sin, God loves you too much to allow you to remain there for any period of time. He will chastise you. A part of His love, like any parent, is to correct you when you are wrong. As a Christian, if you will take steps of correction yourself, it will not be necessary for Him to step in and correct you. First Corinthians 11:31 (KJV) states, *"For if we would judge ourselves, we should not be judged."* I like what Chip Ingram said, "What God's justice demands, His love supplies." All He has demanded, He has already supplied by His love. The way He deals with His children is certainly a more excellent way.

A More Excellent Way

Tracey was distraught and thought to herself, "For twenty years I served and have been faithful to God. I obeyed Him as best I could. Why would He allow me to have a miscarriage? How does this align with His love for me? I don't understand. I cannot wrap my hands around Him letting me carry our first son for six months only to lose him. Why? What did I do wrong? Why did Martha have a healthy baby when all she does is drink, curse, and use God's name in vain? I am puzzled ... why?"

After Paul expounds on spiritual gifts in 1 Corinthians, he ends with these words, *"But covet earnestly the best gifts: and yet shew I unto you a more excellent way"* (1 Cor. 12:31, KJV). Then, continuing under the inspiration of the Holy Spirit, he writes an entire chapter on love (chap. 13). Basically God wants us to know that we can possess wonderful spiritual gifts, but if our gifts are not exercised in love, it means nothing. So anything done without love amounts to nothing! Love is the more excellent way (1 Cor. 12:31).

There is a truth you must hold on to and never, never doubt. It is that our God of love does not do one thing without love. He can't, being that He is love. All He does is in love. Just as He instructs you not to do anything without love, He does not do *anything* without love being behind it. This is important to remember when life snatches the rug out from under your feet, and you are hit with a tragedy or hardship. It is important to know when we don't understand or see Him working in the way we desire for Him to work. It is important when we don't feel His presence at all. Just as Mary and Martha did not understand His delay when their brother Lazarus died, Jesus had a greater purpose in mind. As much as He loved these three, He loved all the rest too who would witness the glory of His father in raising Lazarus from the dead. You must settle in your heart once and for all that God loves *you*! Yes, it is easy to believe He loves others, but you must grasp hold of this truth—Jesus, loves you! You are one of His prized possessions. He delights in you (Ps.18:19)! Let that soak in for a moment. He truly loves you; yes, you—flaws and all. He lets you know how much He loves you in the following Scriptures:

"My sheep hear My voice, and I know them, and they follow Me. And I give them eternal life, and they shall never perish; neither shall anyone snatch them out of My hand. My Father, who has given them to Me, is greater than all; and no one is able to snatch them out of My Father's hand. I and My Father are one" (John 10:27–30, NKJV).

"What shall we say about such wonderful things as these? If God is for us, who can ever be against us? Since he did not spare even his own Son but gave him up for us all, won't he also give us everything else? Who dares accuse us whom God has chosen for his own? No one—for God himself has given us right standing with himself. Who then will condemn us? No one—for Christ Jesus died for us and was raised to life for us, and he is sitting in the place of honor at God's right hand, pleading for us. Can anything ever separate us from Christ's love? Does it mean he no longer loves us if we have trouble or calamity, or are persecuted, or hungry, or destitute, or in danger, or threatened with death? (As the Scriptures say, "For your sake we are killed every day; we are being slaughtered like sheep.") No, despite all these things, overwhelming victory is ours through Christ, who loved us. And I am convinced that nothing can ever separate us from God's love. Neither death nor life, neither angels nor demons, neither our fears for today nor our worries about tomorrow—not even the powers of hell can separate us from God's love. No power in the sky above or in the earth below—indeed, nothing in all creation will ever be able to separate us from the love of God that is revealed in Christ Jesus our Lord" (Rom. 8:31–39, NLT).

From God's point of view, neither Satan nor anything else can separate us from His love. You need to get to the point where you have the same view as Him. Nothing can cause you to doubt His love for you or cause you to "fall out of love" with Him. Look at what He is saying. Is there anyone, seen or unseen, that can separate you from Him? No! These circumstances may cause separation in other human relationships, but not God's with you. It is when these things take place, and you do not doubt His love for you that He will take them and use them to draw you closer to Him. You are overwhelmingly victorious in the grace Christ gives you to overcome. Only Christ is able to bring sweetness out of bitterness, strength out of weakness, triumph out of tragedy, and blessing out of heartbreak.

You too must be convinced there is nothing that can separate you from His love. Nothing—sin, death—nothing! This verse also lets us know more about His love for you:

1. Since you belong to God, no one can successfully come up against you. No lesser power can defeat His will for you.
2. If, by the sacrificial death of Christ, God has taken care of your worst problem of sin, will He not also take care of the minor problems you face ("*Won't he also give us everything else?*").
3. Who can bring a charge against you? Who can condemn you? No one, for God is the Judge and He has declared you innocent through the shed blood of Jesus Christ! Jesus paid your sin debt fully and forever. No charge can ever be brought against you again.
4. Even the persecutions and tribulations that can end human relationships will not separate you from His love. Such things as: trouble, calamity, persecution, hunger, being destitute, in danger, or threatened with death. All of these things that cause stress, distress, affliction, anguish, brutality, nakedness, defenselessness, or threat of danger cannot snatch you away from His unconditional love.
5. The extremes that exist in the universe cannot separate you from His love:
    a. Death or life—you will still be in His loving presence.
    b. Angels or demons—cannot affect or interfere with His love.
    c. Present or future—whether unexpected things that invade your life now or future things that would threaten you cannot plug up the fountain of love flowing to you.
    d. Powers—earthly authorities in power or Satan, who is an unseen power, cannot overrule or stop His love for you.

e. Height or depth—nothing above or beneath can separate you from His love.

Paul could not find anything that could come between you and the God that loves you. Accept this truth and be secure in His love. The question now comes to you. On your behalf will you allow anything to separate your love for Him? He is a gentleman and has given you a free will. He desires for you to choose Him as He has chosen you. Will you allow any of these things to cause a separation in your love for Him? What extremes can be listed to cause you to separate yourself from Him? Will it be anything that concerns your relationship with your spouse, family, friends, or others? Something will always try to come between you.

"Then He said to another, 'Follow Me.' But he said, 'Lord, let me first go and bury my father.' Jesus said to him, 'Let the dead bury their own dead, but you go and preach the kingdom of God.' And another also said, 'Lord, I will follow You, but let me first go and bid them farewell who are at my house.' But Jesus said to him, 'No one, having put his hand to the plow, and looking back, is fit for the kingdom of God'" (Luke 9:59–62, NKJV).

The person in this passage referred to Jesus as Lord but said, "Let me *first* go …" If Jesus is Lord, then He must be first. To say He is first in your life and then insert something that you feel must be first, is a contradiction. He was allowing something else to take precedence over the Lord's call on his life. This may seem strong to you and not compassionate, since it was his father, but it was stated to make a strong point. There are things in life that are not wrong to do, but if they are put first before your commitment to Jesus, then they become wrong. The words "not fit for the kingdom" are in reference to service and not salvation. Jesus Christ must be allowed to reign in the heart without other rivals. All other loves and all other loyalties must be secondary. He has told you how committed He is to you. Will you at least make a decision to be committed to Him as well? If you are already committed, that is great. Now purpose to continue in your commitment no matter what comes. There are so many things on our daily agendas, but love is the more excellent way.

An additional aspect of God's love should be addressed. It is when He must chastise His children. To chastise means to discipline. Sometimes the discipline is rebuke or punishment. Other times the discipline involves teaching and training. A loving parent will instruct and teach a child in the right way to go, but when that child disobeys, the parent, in love, will correct the child. We respect parents for doing so. How much more should God be respected when He disciplines. *"As many as I love, I rebuke and chasten. Therefore be zealous and repent"* (Rev. 3:19, NKJV). His chastisement is always for our good. It is not out of revenge or trying to retaliate for disobedience. If you have always had a picture of a furious God that was ready to strike anyone who got out of line, this may be hard for you to fathom.

"And have you forgotten the encouraging words God spoke to you as his children? He said, 'My child, don't make light of the Lord's discipline, and don't give up when he corrects you. For the Lord disciplines those he loves, and he punishes each one he accepts as his child.' As you endure this divine discipline, remember that God is treating you as his own children. Who ever heard of a child who is never disciplined by its father? If God doesn't discipline you as he does all of his children, it means that you are illegitimate and are not really his children at all. Since we respected our earthly fathers who disciplined us, shouldn't we submit even more to the discipline of the Father of our spirits, and live forever? For our earthly fathers disciplined us for a few years, doing the best they knew how. But God's discipline is always good for us, so that we might share in his holiness. No discipline is enjoyable while it is happening—it's painful! But afterward there will be a peaceful harvest of right living for those who are trained in this way. So take a new grip with your tired hands and strengthen your weak knees" (Heb. 12:5–12, NLT).

Divine discipline is an evidence of divine love. When the Lord chastens (disciplines) you there are two wrong responses: (1) to ignore His instruction when disciplined, and (2) to become discouraged and give up when He corrects you. Instead, let the discipline remind you that you are a true child of His who is being trained into maturity. Respect Him for loving you that much to not let you go astray. Remember, He is a God of love who does not do one thing without love being the motivation for it. *"God's law was given so that all people could see how sinful they were. But as people sinned more and more, God's wonderful grace became more abundant"* (Rom. 5:20, NLT).

When you develop this understanding of God's love, and it becomes a conviction of your heart, your life will change. You will not be tossed back and forth wondering, "He loves me; He loves me not. He loves me; He loves me not." When a trial comes into your life, and you experience some form of suffering, you will not automatically believe it is because of something you did wrong. Or you will not so rapidly conclude He is mad and striking out at you. You will know this situation was allowed by God for some benefit. He is working out something for good. Now this may seem morbid when someone's life is taken or something traumatic happens, but within there still needs to be a silent conviction that God is doing something that is not understood at this point. He cannot do any evil, so somehow good will result, although you do not have eyes to see it. Everything is done in love, for love is the more excellent way.

This is my prayer for you when you do not understand God's love and why something is being allowed to touch your life:

> *For this reason I bow my knees to the Father of our Lord Jesus Christ, from whom the whole family in heaven and earth is named, that He would grant you, according to the riches of His glory, to be strengthened with might through His Spirit in the inner man, that Christ may dwell in your hearts through faith; that you, being rooted and grounded in love, may be able to comprehend with all the saints what is the width and length and depth and height—to know the love of Christ which passes knowledge; that you may be filled with all the fullness of God. Now to Him who is able to do exceedingly abundantly above all that we ask or think, according to the power that works in us, to Him be glory in the church by Christ Jesus to all generations, forever and ever. Amen (Eph. 3:14–21, NKJV).*

When you continue on this path of love, you may have to discipline yourself or do things that will not make sense to the ones you love. Just be mindful to do everything in love and not out of selfish ambition. What you do at home with your spouse and with your family and friends should always be bathed in His love. It may not make sense all the time, but keep your focus on Him. Learn to let Him fight your battles. There will be times when your love will be questioned or not received. There will be times when you feel taken advantage of. There

Paula Harris

will be times when you just do not even want to be around a certain person. You keep self under the control of His Spirit and trust Him to handle what you cannot. Yet in all of these conditions, the good and the bad, love is the more excellent way. Let love be a part of all you do. This is what God does, and you are called to do the same. Let this be the passionate purpose behind all you do.

Passionate Purpose

Doris got down on her knees and could not thank God enough for the changes He had brought into her life. As her cheeks were muffled in the palms of her hands, she began to cry. How could she have been so mean and full of anger before? How could she hold onto bitterness for so long? Why didn't she let go sooner? The love of Jesus had transformed her into a new person. Not only did she surprisingly love others, she found she liked herself. Many were beginning to comment on how she was so kind and gentle and loving. "If they only knew," she often thought.

First Corinthians 16:14 says, *"Do everything in love."* Wow, the word "everything" leaves nothing out. There is so much corruption in the world of what love is and how it operates in relationships—seems like the days of Noah! What is needed is for you and me to believe God and make a choice to live in accordance with His will. Romans 12:1–2 states, *"I beseech you therefore, brethren, by the mercies of God, that ye present your bodies a living sacrifice, holy, acceptable unto God, which is your reasonable service. And be not conformed to this world: but be ye transformed by the renewing of your mind, that ye may prove what is that good, and acceptable, and perfect, will of God."*

This book was written to renew your mind with what God has declared and designed love to be. In agreeing with God and not going along with what the world says, your mind will be continually renewed. All behavior begins in the mind. You have a thought that leads into an action that leads into a habit that leads into a lifestyle. So in renewing your mind you can have a renewed lifestyle as well. By living differently than what you see in the world, you will be shining a light on what God says is His good and acceptable and perfect will. Not only will you show forth His "love light" in the world, you will see and know for yourself that His way is perfect and so much better than anything the world can offer. When others see your joy, deliverance, and healthy relationships, they will desire to have the same. You can see how this can cause a ripple effect just by one person deciding to let his or her light shine. It would be the same as being in a very dark room where you could not see the face of another. Then someone strikes a match, and how that little light gives ambience to the entire room. This is what it will be like if you continue on this journey from the book to your own home, to your extended family, then to friends and others in your communities. Letting your personal love light shine is what our Lord intended for you from the beginning of time. Can you imagine what it would be like if all Christians were to let their love lights shine? Can you picture the blinding light that would penetrate the darkness?

It is easy to see why Satan has an all-out war to distort your view of God's love for you, your view of how to accept and love others, and how to even love yourself properly. It is a war that will be fought until you reach heaven. In truth, Christ has already won the war; you are just fighting individual battles until our Commander in Chief returns to put the enemy away for good. You have already been declared victorious in Christ!

Over and over again in this book you have focused on Matthew 22:37–40. These are commandments from our Lord on how He has designed love to work in relationships. Much has been discussed in regard to the contrast between divine love and human love. In each section, some aspect of love was covered:

In Part 1, "Lost Love," you saw how human love can end up hurting you deeply. Therefore, you need to be careful not to develop a hostile, unforgiving heart, where you try to protect yourself from ever being hurt by love again. This part focused on the problems you may face in relationships.

In Part 2, "Loyal Love," you saw God's original design and plan for love and how no earthly love can ever be a substitute for His divine love. You were created to be in a love relationship with God. His love is unconditional and not based on your performance. He did not just say He loved you; He proved it by the sacrificial death of His Son, Jesus Christ, on your behalf. This part focused on your vertical love relationship with God.

In Part 3, "Love Lens," you saw more deeply what love looks like when it is in operation in the life of a Christian. You saw how God has made it possible for His children to extend agápe love to others even when it is difficult. This part focused on the horizontal love relationship with others.

In Part 4, "Love Light," you saw what was required to have your love light shine in a dark world where relationships are under attack. A challenge was given for you to let your personal light shine. Several disciplines were covered that will safeguard the relationships you develop. This part focused on practical ways to live out your relationship with God and others.

Much has been explained about God's agápe love. John 13:17 states, *"Now that you know these things, you will be blessed if you do them."* I know this is a large amount of information to digest. I suggest you keep the book in a convenient place so you can refer to it when needed. You can bless others with the information contained herein too, for all of us are always involved in relationships.

Before bringing the book to an end, I felt led to give you some additional easy steps that can be followed to bless your relationships and to let your "love light" shine brightly. They are easy to remember and vital in learning *to love from the inside out*. They will make you better equipped to *receive* and *give* love. So now when a challenge occurs in one of your relationships, remember the three *p*'s and the three *h*'s regarding agápe love. Switch from the three *p*'s to the three *h*'s as quickly as possible when interacting with others. Soon you will develop a lifestyle that will bring enjoyment to you and glory to God.

Be careful to avoid the three p's and to passionately pursue the three h's:

Pride, Perception, and Performance:

- **Pride**—Avoid having an excessive opinion of your own importance. Don't look down on others as if they are inferior to you. This will lead to loneliness.
- **Perception**—Avoid doing whatever it takes to be viewed favorably by others more so than Jesus. This will drain you.

- **Performance**—Avoid working hard so others will not reject you. This can lead to resentment.

Humility, Honesty, and Holy Spirit: *(These three are the opposite of three listed above.)*

- **Humility**—Do extend grace to others and be long-suffering with them; treat them in the way you desire to be treated. You will become compassionate.
- **Honesty**—Do be yourself—genuine and truthful, not letting others make you feel ashamed for not being perfect in their eyes. You will become free!
- **Holy Spirit**—Do yield control to Him, knowing there is no need to work for approval, for Jesus has secured your approval for all eternity. You will have joy.

We will not stand before Jesus to be judged regarding our salvation, but we will stand before Him regarding our obedience to the two commands we have focused on. God's Word further says: *"For other foundation can no man lay than that is laid, which is Jesus Christ. Now if any man build upon this foundation gold, silver, precious stones, wood, hay, stubble; Every man's work shall be made manifest: for the day shall declare it, because it shall be revealed by fire; and the fire shall try every man's work of what sort it is. If any man's work abide which he hath built thereupon, he shall receive a reward. If any man's work shall be burned, he shall suffer loss: but he himself shall be saved; yet so as by fire. Know ye not that ye are the temple of God, and that the Spirit of God dwelleth in you? If any man defile the temple of God, him shall God destroy; for the temple of God is holy, which temple ye are"* (1 Cor. 3:11–17, KJV).

Since we have learned all that the law and prophets taught is summarized in the two commandments, it behooves us to live in obedience to them. All of our own efforts to fulfill them will be considered wood, hay, and stubble. All of our obedience to them in the power of the Holy Spirit will be counted as gold, silver, and precious stones. It is the human efforts that will not last and be burned. It is what God does within us that will stand in the end. The exciting thing is that He will fulfill what He has called you personally to do!

Dropped but Not Broken

You may close these pages, but please do not close your heart. Letting your "Love Light" shine is a commitment that is necessary until Jesus comes back to take you home. He desires for you to believe Him and take Him at His Word. He desires those who will be used of Him to reach others. With this in mind, I am confident you will have a passionate purpose to know and share God's agápe love with others. Decide now to have a passionate purpose to **receive** and **give** *love from the inside out.*

When you think about our Father, it is amazing that He pays attention to the tiniest details. Think of the veins along with the intricately placed colors on a butterfly's wing. Think of the flight pattern of a hummingbird. Think of how everything that is needed to grow a large oak tree is contained in one small seed. Think of how He has, by His divine power, given you everything you need to live a godly life in this perverse world. *"By his divine power, God has given us everything we need for living a godly life. We have received all of this by coming to know him, the one who called us to himself by means of his marvelous glory and excellence"* (2 Pet. 1:3, NLT). We have no excuse for why we cannot live as He commands.

So many Christians are angry and upset, holding onto unforgiveness, bitterness, and selfishness. The Word of God reminds us that love will wax cold. *"And because iniquity shall abound, the love of many shall wax cold"* (Matt. 24:12, KJV). Will you go forth and allow the warmth of your love to penetrate another so his or her love does not wax cold? Jesus will **never** stop loving you and will be there to lift you up should the bottom fall out from under you. Will you be a funnel of His love to lift another up when the bottom falls out from under his or her life? If you will step out, He will provide everything that you need to mend, heal, restore, or build up the relationships in your life. Remember, love *never* fails!

Completing this book has been the basis of a call to have a "passionate purpose." Now I am gently asking you to join all of us women who have made a decision to spread the love of God. This is what God has clearly instructed in His Word and has Himself commanded all of His children to do. Julie Clinton once said, "If relationships with God and others are what matter most in life, we need to ask ourselves what we're doing to strengthen these closest relationships. Often, we're so caught up in life that we inadvertently put our connections with others on autopilot, hoping that the relationships will still be intact when life settles down a bit. Because life rarely settles down, we can go weeks, months, and even years without investing time in the people we love most."

My sister, I would like to invite you to be a part of a worldwide challenge to live out God's agápe love from the inside out. You have learned foundational truths, but putting them into practice continuously may appear to be a big challenge—this is a whole new way of living! To reach the correct destination, you must get on the right road. Transformed Worldwide Ministries is committed to expounding, exhorting, and empowering through the Word of God so others may know Jesus Christ and be transformed into His likeness. *"As for me, I will behold thy face in righteousness: I shall be satisfied, when I awake, with thy likeness"* (Ps. 17:15, KJV). This is the passionate call of my life. There is such joy in assisting others in learning how to love Jesus and others. I trust you will let our ministry team come alongside of you by going to our website (www.twmforjesus.org) and signing up to receive continual encouragement and any other lesson material you desire. An annual conference is held to build you up as well. The motto of our ministry is, "Reaching Women and the Ones They Love." It would bring our staff such delight to be able to reach out to you personally and provide the support you need.

This sisterhood is one whereby we will encourage and strengthen one another on this continued love journey. We have a lot of the same concerns and can share insight and get our questions answered one with another.

Daily, women are being dropped, but they (along with you) need to know it does not mean they are broken. Let's love from the inside out!

Finally, brethren, farewell. Become complete. Be of good comfort, be of one mind, live in peace; and the God of love and peace will be with you (2 Cor. 13:11, NKJV).

I am rejoicing over your decision to live a divine life of love. Come; let the issues that have plagued us for years be healed as we touch the hem of Jesus's garment together (Matt. 14:36). I look forward to meeting you at the feet of Jesus.

Smile; Jesus loves you!

Resources

Come love from the inside out! We have a host of lesson materials and encouragement that will inspire you as you passionately try to live each day loving Jesus and others.

Go to our website for more information. I would enjoy hearing from you as well.

www.twmforjesus.org

paula@twmforjesus.org

Reference

Walvoord, J. F., R. B. Zuck & Dallas Theological Seminary. *The Bible Knowledge Commentary: An Exposition of the Scriptures* (1 John 1:1). Wheaton, IL: Victor Books, 1983.

Endnotes

1. Spurgeon, C. H. *Morning and Evening: Daily Readings* (Complete and unabridged; New modern edition.). Peabody, MA: Hendrickson Publishers, 2006.
2. Hardman, S. G., & Moody, D. L. *Thoughts for the Quiet Hour*. Willow Grove, PA: Woodlawn Electronic Publishing, 1998.
3. Manser, Martin H. *The Westminster Collection of Christian Quotations*, pg. 299. Louisville, KY: Westminster John Knox Press, 2001.
4. Dr. Phil. *Letting Go of Love*. www.drphil.com/articles/article/172. Peteski Productions, Inc., 2009.
5. Hardman, S. G., & Moody, D. L. *Thoughts for the Quiet Hour*. Willow Grove, PA: Woodlawn Electronic Publishing, 1998.
6. Young, Sarah. *Jesus Calling*. Brentwood, TN: Integrity Publishers, a division of Integrity Media, Inc., 2004.